BARRIERE LIBRARY

T014784667

599.522
Busch, Robert, 1953–
Gray whales : wandering
giants / Robert H. Busch.

D0117999

Gray Whales
Wandering Giants

Robert H. Busch

ORCA BOOK PUBLISHERS

Thompson-Nicola Regional District
Library System
300 - 465 VICTORIA STREET
KAMLOOPS, B.C.   V2C 2A9

To Genie, with much love
R.H.B.

Copyright © 1998 Robert H. Busch

No part of this book may be reproduced, stored in a retrieval system, or transmitted, in any form or by any means, without the prior written permission of the publisher, except by a reviewer who may quote brief passages in review.

Canadian Cataloguing in Publication Data
Busch, Robert, 1953 –
Gray whales

Includes bibliographical references and index.
ISBN 1-55143-114-9

1. Gray Whale. I. Title.

QL737.C425B87 1998 599.5'22 C97-911051-3

Library of Congress Catalog Card Number: 97-81071

Orca Book Publishers gratefully acknowledges the support of our publishing programs provided by the following agencies: the Department of Canadian Heritage, The Canada Council for the Arts, and the British Columbia Ministry of Small Business, Tourism and Culture.

Design by Christine Toller and Susan Adamson
Printed and bound in Canada

Orca Book Publishers
PO Box 5626, Station B
Victoria, BC Canada
V8R 6S4

Orca Book Publishers
PO Box 468
Custer, WA USA
98240-0468

98 99 00   5 4 3 2 1

1014784667

Table of Contents

Preface

The first sight of them makes you gasp in awe.

On my first whale sighting, there were six of us crammed into a Zodiac, each wearing a bright orange inflatable survival suit in case we tipped into the chilly waters off Vancouver Island.

We had spotted the misty blow of a whale near to shore and had bounced our way over three-meter (ten-foot) waves to get closer. Suddenly, twelve meters (forty feet) of whale burst out of the water, hung in the air for a second, and then crashed back into the waves, sending out a huge spray of water that drenched us all. Some of that water entered our open mouths, caught in mid-gasp at one of nature's most spectacular sights.

The wonder that humans express at the great whales runs very deep, and the affection that man has for the gray whale is especially intense. No other large whale regularly allows humans to touch it, and no other whale is watched by so many people each year, for the coastal migration of the gray whale along the western edge of North America brings it into the sight of millions of people.

What is it about the whales that stirs us so?

Part of the attraction is the sheer size of whales, their almost unique ability to make us feel very small and very humble. The Elizabethan naturalist Bartholomew put it well when he said that "for greatness of body ... [the whale] seemeth an island."

Another part of our interest in whales is derived from the tenuous thing called freedom, for the sight of many a wild and free animal moves something inside us, plucking those same internal strings that make us want to get out to the country on weekends or go away on vacations.

Or perhaps it is something deeper, something locked within the Freudian mysteries that slosh around inside our heads. Our own bodies are sixty-five percent water, and so it might be that whales symbolize in a very big way our own watery makeup and origins, for eons ago we too sprang from the sea. To some psychologists, our affection for whales is explained by their status as "the ultimate phallic symbol." To anyone who has watched a whale dive smoothly into the sea, engulfed by its liquid caress, the analogy seems especially apt. Or is it because whales, like us, are mammals, and that deep inside us we feel a biological kinship with our huge warm-blooded cousins?

There is also the unassailable fact that humans are often drawn to evil, and to many early writers, a huge menacing whale was the epitomy of evil. The biblical story of Jonah swallowed by the whale has Jonah crying "out of the belly of hell." Pieter Brueghel the Elder used the open mouth of the whale to represent the gates of hell, a vicious symbolism for so benign a creature.

Whatever the attraction, mankind has had a long relationship with the whale, beginning with our efforts to harpoon it and continuing today with our efforts to save it.

Jacques Cousteau calls the whale simply "the most astonishing animal the earth has ever known."

And once one has had a close encounter of the friendly kind with a great whale, it is unlikely that he or she will ever forget the experience. Veteran whale-watcher Roger Payne says that whales "tend to lodge in the breasts of people—sometimes they lodge cross-wise where they stick for life."

Today, whale-watching is big business, with thousands of people each year taking to sporty Zodiacs or sedate cruisers in order to get close to the huge beasts.

But what do they see? All too often, all they get is a mere glimpse of a tail disappearing beneath the waves or of a distant whale spouting a cloud of mist into the air. In 1851, Herman Melville, author of *Moby Dick,* wrote "there is no earthly way of finding out precisely what the whale really looks like." In 1972, Jacques Cousteau wrote that "man knows very little about these giants of the sea." More recently, Charles "Stormy" Mayo, director of the Center for Coastal Studies in Provincetown, Massachusetts, has stated that we see "maybe ten minutes, all told, out of what may be a forty-year life of the whale, in thousands of miles of ocean."

This book is an attempt to extend that glimpse, to show all of the beast; in short, to reveal the fascinating creature that biologists call *Eschrichtus robustus* and that tourists call gray whales, the friendliest of the amazing whales.

Robert H. Busch,
December 1997

Chapter One   The Nature of the Beast

And God created great whales, and every living creature ... and God saw that it was good.
— Genesis 1:21-23

Evolution of the Gray Whale

Like many people, I have spent some time in recent years tracing my ancestry, engaging in the age-old quest for knowing who I am and where I came from. Biologists have done the same thing with various whale species, and in the case of the gray whale, they have come up with some surprising ancestors indeed.

When you look at a whale today, its glistening bulk the epitome of streamlining, it is hard to believe that whales have developed from four-legged land animals that lived millions of years ago. About ninety million years ago, the first mammal-like reptile appeared on Earth, and it in turn evolved into a larger animal with an elongated snout.

Whales probably evolved from dog-sized, long-snouted animals known as mesonychids. According to the fossil evidence of mesonychid teeth, the animals lived on both animals and plant matter. These terrestrial ancestors are thought to have invaded brackish estuaries about fifty-five million years ago, evolving into a half-land, half-water creature known as *Protocetus*. As its success in the water increased, *Protocetus* evolved into a suborder of wholly marine animals known as the archeocetes, which first appeared about fifty million years ago during the late Eocene Period.

The archeocetes were carnivorous beasts which prowled the margins of the seas, rather than venture into deep water. They looked rather snake-like, with elongated

FACING PAGE: *The mighty tail flukes of the gray whale, photographed in Ritchie, BC.* (George Fifield, © Vancouver Island Postcards)

bodies and crocodile-like heads. They reached their zenith about forty million years ago, and died out around thirty million years ago.

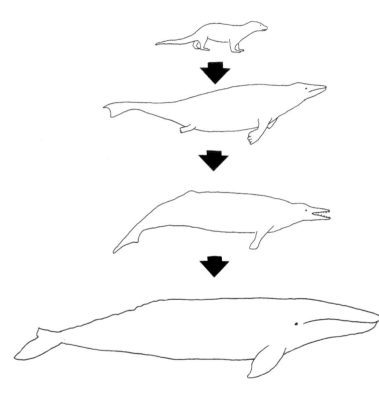

Evolution of the gray whale.

As the evolution of the archeocetes accelerated, it was accompanied by a number of physiological changes which allowed a permanent marine existence. Firstly, the original external body hair was lost to reduce drag in the water; in today's gray whales, a few bristly hairs on the snout and lower jaw are the remnants of the early fur coat worn by the whale's ancestors. Secondly, the front limbs evolved into flippers. Today's whales still possess flippers with four or five finger-like extensions, the de-volved equivalent of human hands. The hind limbs atro-phied and finally disappeared altogether; in modern whales, the bones of vestigial hind limbs can still be found bur-ied deep within muscle tissue in the hind quarters. Ex-ternal genitalia were absorbed to reduce friction in the water, for drag of any sort slows down the animal. The nostrils moved from a frontal position to the top of the head, enabling the animal to keep most of its bulk un-derwater yet still breathe. And perhaps most importantly of all, blubber developed, a crucial adaptation for a large sea creature, for sea water saps heat from bodies twenty times faster than air. Some whale embryos today have four limbs, external genitalia, and nostrils at the end of a snout, remnants of their ancestors' appearance.

The result of these evolutionary changes was an animal known as *Pakicetus*, a whale-like genus discovered in 1980 which looks very much like today's toothed whales. Many biologists think it was a link between the archeocetes-type of creature and modern whales. *Pakicetus* was probably the first whale-like animal that ventured into deep water.

From here, the family tree of the whale begins to split into two branches: the baleen whales and the toothed whales. Baleen whales do not possess teeth, but have a series of long plates called baleen which hang from the upper jaw and screen out food. Toothed whales possess long teeth used to hold prey.

Fetuses of modern baleen whales retain tooth buds below the gum line, suggesting that baleen whales evolved from toothed whales. If this is correct, and recent DNA work seems to confirm it, the toothed whales were the first to develop from *Pakicetus*, and from the toothed whales came the first baleen whale. It appeared during the middle Oligocene Period, about twenty-eight million years ago.

Gray whales are baleen whales. Many biologists believe that gray whales are the most primitive of the baleen whales and perhaps were the first to evolve, pointing out that they possess an underdeveloped dorsal fin, underdeveloped baleen, a small head, relatively few throat grooves, and breed in shallow coastal water. Others believe that these are secondary characteristics, pointing to an advanced and specialized type of whale.

The first fossil gray whales date to the late Pleistocene Epoch, about 100,000 years ago. Archeologists predict that even older forms may still be found dating back ten million years to the Miocene or late Pliocene. Fossils of gray whales show that their form has changed very little in the past 100,000 years. They are, in fact, a living fossil, one of those unique species whose evolution has come to a complete and successful conclusion.

The identity of the whale's closest living relative would come as a surprise to most people. Researchers at Rutgers University have found that the structure of whale blood serum most closely resembles that of animals known as artiodactyls, a fancy name for hooved animals such as cows, pigs, and sheep.

Recently, biologists have used a technique called molecular phylogenetics to pinpoint the whales' closest living relative even further. It is the hippopotamus, which shares ninety percent of the molecular sequences found in whales. The chubby hippo and the sleek whale—who would have guessed that they're so closely related?

All mysticeti whales have dual blowholes, as shown in this sixteenth-century engraving of the "Miracle of St. Malo." (Archives E.R.L.)

Classification and Taxonomy

For a long time, whales were considered to be giant fishes. Whaling grounds were known as fisheries, and even today whales are often administered by the fisheries departments of governments rather than wildlife departments. It was not until 1693 that John Ray correctly classified whales as mammals. To biologists, the gray whale is known as *Eschrichtius robustus*, a name bestowed in 1864 by J.E. Gray of the British Museum in London. The Latin name commemorates Daniel Eschrichtius, a Danish zoology professor who taught at the University of Copenhagen. The type specimen gray whale was collected in Monterey Bay, California, in 1952.

All whales are classed in the order Cetacea, from the Greek word *ketos*, meaning sea monster. About eighty species of cetaceans have been identified around the world, and new species are still being discovered. Hector's beaked whale, for example, was not discovered until 1980.

Whales are further divided into two suborders. The Odontoceti are the toothed whales such as killer whales and sperm whales. The baleen whales are the Mysticeti, the suborder to which the gray whale belongs. The word Mysticeti is a Greek word meaning mustache, for early naturalists thought that the strips of baleen were on the outside of the jaws like a mustache on a man's upper lip.

The gray whale is classified in its own family, Eschrichtiidae, of which there is only one genus and species, *Eschrichtius robustus*. Gray whales are also known by a number of popular nicknames, including California whale, desert whale, devilfish, hardhead, grayback, mossback, rip-sack, mussel-digger, and clam-digger. In Japan they are called *koku kujira*; in Russia, *seryi kit*.

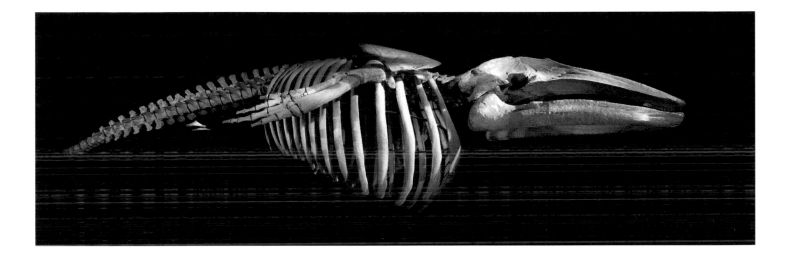

Physical Description

The gray whale is a relatively large whale, twice the length of the killer whale, but half the length of the mighty blue whale. (The largest whale on record is a blue whale caught in 1909 which measured just over thirty three meters [110 feet] long.)

Most adult gray whales are about ten to thirteen meters (35 to 45 feet) long and weigh twenty-two to thirty-eight tonnes (20 to 35 tons). According to whale biologist Ted Walker, "grays exceeding 45 feet [13 meters] are a rarity today." Of 299 whales examined from Russia's Chukotka Peninsula in the 1970s, the average length was 11.5 meters (39 feet).

Female grays tend to be larger than the males. Of 150 gray whales taken off Baja California by Norwegian whalers between 1925 and 1929, only four were estimated to be fifteen meters (50 feet) long; all were females. The record gray whale appears to be a female which measured 15.5 meters (51 feet) long and weighed forty-two tonnes (39 tons).

The general body shape of the gray whale is long and narrow, unlike the bulbous shape that most people seem to expect when they think of whales.

Gray whale skeleton.
(Royal British Columbia Museum)

The long linear shape of the gray whale is evident in this underwater shot taken off the coast of California. (Bob Cranston)

Human

Gray Whale

Blue Whale

Relative size comparison

Gray whales are named for their medium gray color, which is marbled with lighter patches. At the water's surface, gray whales often appear to be a whitish-blue color. In 1957, Russian biologist A. G. Tomilin reported a sighting in the Bering Sea of a partially albino gray whale, whose front half was completely white.

Each whale has a unique skin pigmentation pattern, allowing individuals to be identified. The patterns often include round white markings that result from barnacles that have fallen off. Newborn gray whales are a very dark gray color, which looks almost black in the water. The skin of the gray whale is smooth and feels like a hard-boiled egg without the shell.

Note the throat grooves on this gray whale calf photographed sliding upside down over its mother's back. (Ken Balcomb)

Gray whales do not have teeth, but
have a curtain of baleen which hangs
from the roof of the mouth.
(François Gohier)

The head of a gray whale is long and arches downward. The eyes are brown in color and about the size of an orange. They are located about two meters (6 to 7 feet) behind the tip of the snout. The snout and lower jaw sport a number of short coarse bristles, one clue that the gray whale evolved from well-furred mammals. Typically there are fifty-plus bristles on the top of the snout and twice that on the lower jaw. The curve of the mouth is long and from the side curves down as if in a perpetual grimace. Under the chin, the gray whale has two to five small throat grooves, which expand when the whale is feeding. The whole skull of the gray whale is disproportionately large, and takes up about a fifth of the total body length.

Two large flippers are located about one meter (3 feet) behind and below the eyes. In fish terminology, they would be called pectoral fins, and are used for steering and turning the whale. The skeleton of a gray whale flipper has four long finger-like digits and looks amazingly like that of a human hand. Unlike killer whales, which have a large dorsal fin on their back, the gray only has a series of six to twelve small bumps, called knuckles, located about two-thirds of the way down the back.

Bringing up the rear is the tail, comprised of two large flukes with a notch between them. In an adult gray, the tail flukes can measure over three meters (9 feet) across and can weigh up to 180 kilograms (400 pounds). Unlike the tail of a fish, which is vertical, the tail of a gray whale is horizontal. And unlike the tails of seals or walruses, the tail fin is not a modified hind limb. It is not connected to the spinal column of the whale and is made up primarily of strong connective tissues. Its up-and-down motion provides incredibly powerful forward propulsion.

The bones in a gray whale's flipper look amazingly like those in a human hand. (Richard Beaupied/ The Whale Centre, Tofino, BC)

Inside the gray whale, there are fifty-six vertebrae. Like all mammals, grays have seven cervical vertebrae, the bones that support the short, rigid neck, although from the outside it is hard to tell where the neck stops and the body begins. Picture a long, lean swimming machine and you've pictured the gray whale, one of the sleekest members of the whale family.

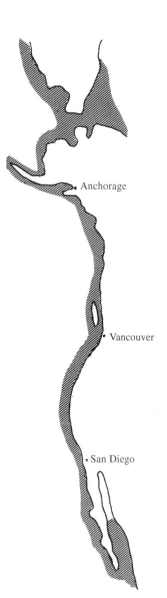

Range of the California gray whale.

The Life Cycle of the Gray Whale

The life cycle of the gray whale is a fascinating story with two settings: the warm lagoons on the coast of Baja California in winter, and the chilly waters off Alaska in summer.

South for the Winter

Each October, the northern ice pushes southward and the days get shorter for gray whales which have spent the summer feeding in the frigid waters of the Bering Sea off the coast of Alaska. It is these cues that send the gray whales south on one of the longest migrations in the animal kingdom. Their target is a handful of lagoons on the west coast of Baja California, some 6,000 kilometers (4,000 miles) to the south. It was long thought that this constituted the longest animal migration in the world, but it is now known that some humpback whales go on even longer treks.

The grays travel both day and night, and average about 125 kilometers (82 miles) per day. By late November they stream through Unimak Pass, in the Aleutian chain of islands off the southwest tip of Alaska. The pass at its narrowest is only eighteen kilometers (12 miles) wide, so at the peak of migration it is completely choked with whales. Most of them swim about 0.5 kilometers (1,700 feet) offshore, in water less than twenty meters (65 feet) deep.

By late December, the whales swim past Vancouver Island, although the winter seas there are too stormy for tourists to whale-watch. The southward migration is also a bit too far out to sea for tourists to spot whales. The grays usually don't come closer to shore until they are off central Oregon. By late December, the whales are usually between Monterey and San Diego, where thousands of residents watch up to two hundred whales a day stream past their shores. Most of the whales swim within 1.5 kilometers (1 mile) of shore.

Near Monterey, about twenty-one kilometers (14 miles) west of Moss Landing, some of the whales leave the migration route and wander into the southern part of Monterey Bay. Then they turn and scoot back to the normal route. No one yet knows why they take this side trip. Part of the reason may be instinct, for each year there are a few whales that give birth in Monterey Bay itself. Newborn gray whale calves are also spotted each year in the Channel Island National Marine Sanctuary further south. Most of the whales migrate past California in December, but each year, a few stragglers can be seen as late as February. These slowpokes encounter northbound whales returning from Baja and often hit the brakes, turn around, and join them. By late December, the main stream of whales reaches the central coast of Baja, about 530 kilometers (350 miles) south of San Diego, where half of the females mate and the other half give birth.

FACING PAGE: *The migration of the gray whale is one of the longest in the animal kingdom.* (François Gohier)

The majority of the California gray whale population is born in the protected waters of Scammon's Lagoon in Baja California. (François Gohier)

Exactly why the gray whale and many other whale species travel to warmer climes to breed and give birth is unknown. D.H. Lawrence, in his famous poem "Whales Weep Not," was obviously cognizant of the fact when he wrote:

and in the tropics tremble they with love
and roll with massive, strong desire, like gods.

Reproduction, Whale-Style

The mating process of the gray whale is a strange business that has confused many an observer. Gray whales reach sexual maturity at between five and eleven years of age, averaging about eight years. They reach physical maturity, the point at which their bodies stop growing, at about nineteen.

As one might expect, the sexual organs of a whale are far bigger than the puny organs possessed by humans. In the male gray whale, the penis is a huge organ some 1.5 meters (5 feet) long. It is normally hidden within a slit on the belly of the whale, about halfway between the umbilicus and the anus, and only whips out into view when the whale is sexually excited. The female sexual organs are hidden in an elongated genital slit just forward of the anus. The testes of the male are extra-large, weighing over 20 kilograms (45 pounds) each. (The largest testes in the world belong to the right whale, whose testes are 3 meters [9 feet] long and weigh almost 450 kilograms [1,000 pounds]). Strangely, whale sperm itself is actually smaller than human sperm.

According to Adrian Forsyth, Director of Conservation Biology for Conservation International in Washington, D.C., "There is a clear relationship between how promiscuous animals are, how much sperm males can produce, and the size of the testes relative to body weight." In other words, promiscuous animals have big testes and produce a lot of sperm, because they have to inseminate a lot of females in order for their genes to carry on. Biologists call this "sperm competition."

FACING PAGE: *When gray whales mate, the male's huge pink-colored penis can often be seen at the water's surface.* (Kennan Ward)

For example, chimpanzees, which are very promiscuous, have relatively large testes. Male gorillas, each of which has his own harem of females, have relatively small testes. The rule holds true for whales as well. The gray whale is fairly promiscuous and has relatively large testes. The right whale is highly promiscuous and has huge testes.

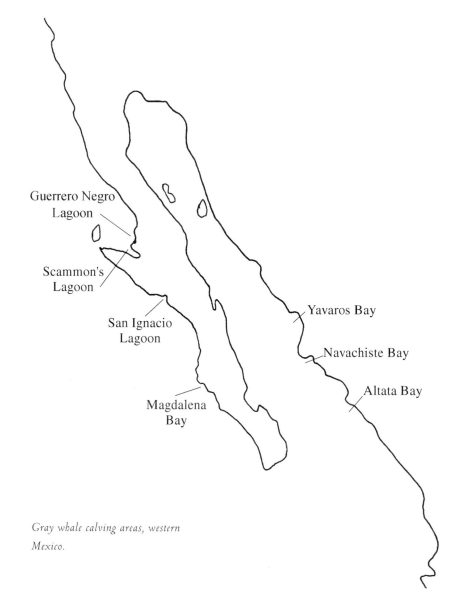

Guerrero Negro
Lagoon

Scammon's
Lagoon

San Ignacio
Lagoon

Yavaros Bay

Navachiste Bay

Altata Bay

Magdalena
Bay

Gray whale calving areas, western Mexico.

As with many mammals, copulation in gray whales is preceded by foreplay. Males are often seen placing a flipper over the back of a female, either as part of foreplay or as an attempt to slow the female down in order to mate. In foreplay, the whales bob up and down and roll over each other, touching each other tenderly with their bodies and their flippers.

To mate, the female usually rolls on her side near the water's surface and her mate joins her, belly to belly. The female often will hold onto the male with her flippers. Sometimes a third male lies across the breeding pair, stabilizing them in rocky seas. If the breeding pair choose to mate a bit deeper underwater, a third male may place himself on the far side of the female to act as a brace.

Copulation often takes place in the early morning and each copulation lasts from only about ten seconds to about two minutes. Usually, pairs will copulate several times in a row for a period of about an hour. Diver Philippe Cousteau watched one copulation and reported: "The preliminaries and foreplay lasted nearly an hour; the animals copulated or attempted copulation about ten times."

Most of the mating occurs in massive bouts that may involve twenty individuals, all of whom change partners frequently during the proceedings. Biologists Steve Swartz and Mary Lou Jones, who observed grays in Baja's San Ignacio Lagoon, observed that "the males seem to be taking turns," although they never observed any fighting between males.

Females escape unwanted Romeos by swimming away rapidly or lying upside down on the water's surface. Jacques Cousteau watched one amorous young male who kept pursuing a female with her calf. The unwilling female "kept pushing away the male with her head," and finally "gave the male a great swat with her tail" and swam away. Why the females accept certain mates and reject other willing males is unknown.

Most of the breeding takes place in four different bays along the coast of Baja: Guerrero Negro, Scammon's, San Ignacio, and Magdalena. Guerrero Negro is the northernmost of these, and lies adjacent to the larger Scammon's Lagoon, a huge complex that stretches forty-five kilometers (30 miles) into the Baja desert. Guerrero Negro Lagoon was named after a whaling ship that went down there in 1858. (As with many shipwrecks, local fishermen believe that there was a fabulous treasure aboard, although since it was just a whaling ship, the story is doubtful.)

San Ignacio Lagoon, known to Mexican fishermen in the 1940s as Ballenas Bay (Whale Bay), lies further south, about 120 kilometers (80 miles) from Scammon's Lagoon. Magdalena Bay is another 270 kilometers (180 miles) south. Over half of all gray whale births take place in Scammon's Lagoon. Magdalena Bay, in comparison, accounts for less than six percent.

Some gray whales round the tip of Baja, stream past Cabo San Lucas, and trek north into the Sea of Cortez (Gulf of California) as far as Bahia de Los Angeles. A small number of grays give birth in the bays of Yavaros, Bahia Navachiste, Bahia Altata, and Bahia Reforma (Santa Maria) on the Mexican mainland across the Sea of Cortez from the tip of Baja.

A rare underwater shot of a pregnant grey whale.
(Kennan Ward)

According to the famous whaler Captain Charles Scammon, gray whales used to swim right up to the northern extremity of the Sea of Cortez. As he wrote in 1874, "Around Consag Island and off Shoal Point near the head of the Gulf of California large numbers of California Gray whales have been seen in March." Today gray whales rarely go farther north in the Gulf than Yavaros Bay.

After mating, the whales leave the lagoons and either swim down to San Ignacio Lagoon or begin the long trip back north. Only the females impregnated the previous year stay in the lagoons for an extended period, in order to give birth and socialize with their new babies. The average mating female only stays for a few weeks; the average pregnant female, for about thirteen weeks.

A Big, Big Baby

The gestation period of the gray whale is about thirteen months, which means that whales impregnated in the lagoons one winter will return a year later to give birth. Most females thus give birth every other year, although birthing two years in a row happens in about one out of every forty-five females. The peak in gray whale births takes place around January 27.

Many females retreat to the furthest reaches of the lagoons to give birth. Others prefer the lagoon entrances, and some even calve at sea just beyond the mouths of the lagoons.

Female gray whales give birth to a single baby, although there is one record of twin fetuses found in a gray whale killed off Russia's Chukotka Peninsula in 1985. Unlike most whales, baby grays are born headfirst. In one well-documented 1975 birth, the mother rolled onto her back at the surface of the water, and the calf was born headfirst into the air. If the baby is born underwater, it instinctively swims to the surface to get its first breath of air, often with the anxious mother pushing it up.

Left: *Baby gray whales are almost pure black in color.* (Bob Cranston)

Right: *Baby gray whales often rest their heads on their mother's broad backs.* (Bob Cranston)

Baby grays are born fully developed, measure about four to five meters long (12 to 16 feet) and weigh 700 to 900 kilograms (1500 to 2000 pounds). The umbilical cord is short and rigid and snaps off easily. Newborns have fetal folds in the skin, from being curled up in a fetal position inside the mother's womb.

Baby gray whales usually suckle less than one hour after birth, although suckle isn't quite the right word. The mother whale actually squirts milk into the baby's mouth using strong muscles that encircle the mammary glands. (The female's nipples are located within two clefts in the skin on each side of the genital slit.) Occasionally, a baby will let go of the nipples too soon, and a jet of milk will shoot out into the water. The mother whale holds the baby to her with her flippers while it nurses.

The newborn gray whale baby drinks between about thirteen and twenty-two liters (3.5 to 6 gallons) of milk per day. The milk is incredibly rich, and is usually between thirty-five and fifty-three percent fat. (Cow milk is only about three to four percent fat.) The milk has about six times the protein content of human milk. Not surprisingly, newborn calves double their weight by the time they leave the lagoons, packing on about ninety kilograms (200 pounds) per day. A mother gray whale will nurse her calf for six to nine months.

Females often let their babies ride on their backs for the first few days. In fact, the calves often use their mothers as huge playgrounds. Biologists Swartz and Jones noted, "They swim onto her rotund back and slide off, roll across her massive tail stock, and pummel her with their leaping back-flops and belly-flops." The calves sometimes mistake big tour boats for their mothers, and attempt to rub against the boats, to the delight of the people on board. After they get a bit bigger, the young calves like to lie at right angles to their mothers, with their heads resting across their mothers' broad backs.

The young whales spend a lot of time in play, surfing on the waves and sometimes rapidly spinning in one spot at up to sixty revolutions per minute. They begin breaching (leaping out of the water onto their sides or backs) within the first few weeks of life. Sometimes they will use objects in the lagoons as toys. Calves have been seen grabbing the round floats on kelp in their mouths, releasing them underwater so

FACING PAGE: *A gray whale mother and calf often tenderly rub against each other.*
(François Gohier)

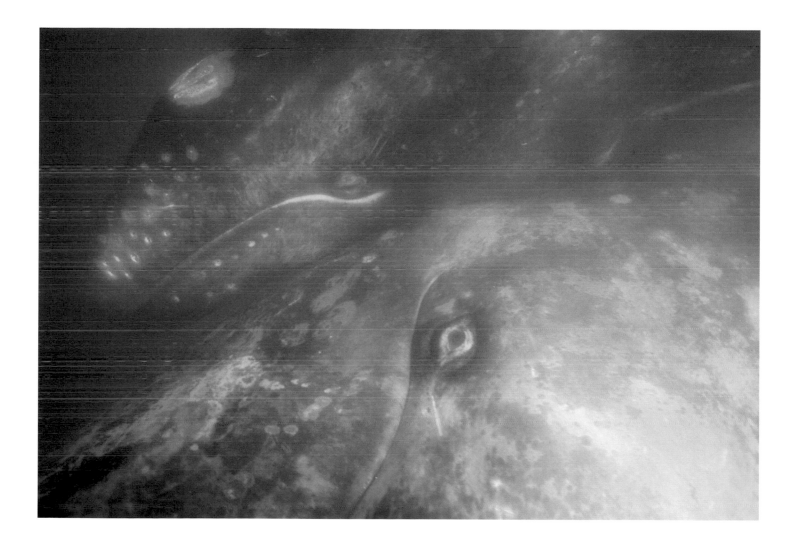

they shoot to the surface, and then pulling them underwater again. (I once watched a family of otters doing the same thing with a buoyant piece of wood.) All of these types of play help burn off excess energy.

As the calves get a bit older, up to twenty mother and calf pairs will get together to play and socialize, the whale equivalent of human mothers with toddlers gathering in nursery schools. The nursery lagoon then becomes a tranquil place filled with females and calves, with a great deal of physical contact among the whales. Swartz and Jones described it well: "The calves run around chasing each other, playing, and the females loll around, splashing and jumping ... Calves also appear to frolic in Jacuzzi-like 'bubble-bursts' created when their mothers release explosions of air underwater which boil to the surface."

The mothers teach their young to stay away from the big males, and will slap them with their flippers to warn of danger or reprimand them. Jacques Cousteau witnessed one such reprimand when a baby whale left its mother's side and approached the side of Cousteau's boat: "The mother immediately went after the calf, pushed it far away from the ship, and then struck it several times with her flippers."

Swartz and Jones observed just how the babies gain strength needed for swimming by "facing into the strong incoming or outgoing tidal currents. They swim strenuously as though on a treadmill, going nowhere but getting a valuable workout."

The mother often strokes her baby with her broad flippers and rubs her body against it in a tender show of affection. She will also strongly defend her baby, as many unfortunate humans have discovered. Captain Charles Scammon noted in 1874 that "this species of whale manifests the greatest affection for its young." He also quickly learned that "the parent animal, in her frenzy, will chase the boats, and overtaking them, will overturn them with her head, or dash them in pieces with a stroke of her ponderous flukes." It is no wonder that early whalers knew the gray whale as the devilfish.

As Scammon noted, "the mother ... may momentarily lose sight of her little one. Instantly she will stop and 'sweep' around in search." And woe to anyone who comes between a mother gray whale and her calf. Unfortunately, many reckless humans have tried.

In 1956, heart specialist Paul Dudley White tried to implant an electrocardiograph lead in a female gray whale to record her heartbeat. (I have no idea why he wanted this unusual bit of information.) Clyde Rice, who assisted White, says, "His idea was to shoot an arrow into a whale with these instruments attached." White did not listen to Rice's warnings about the aggressiveness of female gray whales and shot an arrow into the back of one female, who had a calf alongside. Her reaction to the shot was immediate. "The whale's tail flukes came down," Rice says, "and we got smashed to pieces." The boat's rudder and propeller were sheared off and the hull was splintered. "Thousands and thousands of dollars worth of gear went down to the bottom. We had to swim to shore," Rice says. White quickly called off the experiment.

In the 1960s, a group of thoughtless Hollywood photographers tried to get exciting film footage of angry female gray whales by throwing cherry bombs into the tranquil Baja lagoons. As might be expected, the whales simply fled when faced with such bizarre enemies.

A few years later, a team of Jacques Cousteau's divers thoughtlessly pushed one female gray whale too far, chasing her for hours in a Zodiac boat. She turned, breached, and landed on top of the boat, destroying it. One of the divers came out of the encounter with a dislocated knee; the others, with a greater respect for the power of the gray whale.

Juvenile gray whales soon get a thick coating of barnacles and lice. Note the diver in the background.
(Bob Cranston)

Swartz and Jones also observed one of the most fascinating examples of the whales' protective nature when a calf got stuck on a shallow sandbar:

> Instantly, an adult whale we took to be the calf's mother surged out of the channel and beached itself beside the calf. Seconds later another whale beached itself on the other side, sandwiching the calf between the two adults. Both adults thereupon raised their heads and flukes, pivoted with the calf between them, and slid smoothly back into the channel.

In San Ignacio Lagoon, where Swartz and Jones did all their work, eighty-one percent of the grays stay in the lagoon for a week or less. The lagoon is actually in a constant state of flux, with some whales entering and some leaving. In one seven-hour survey, 341 entered the lagoon and 185 left.

Some cows return to the same lagoons year after year to give birth, and others use a different one each time. Some visit different lagoons within a single winter season. Many use San Ignacio as a meeting place or staging area before heading north, including cows and calves from Guerrero Negro and Scammon's lagoons.

In San Ignacio Lagoon, most females prefer to give birth in the upper part of the lagoon, where the water is four meters (14 feet) deep. At the peak of the mating season, San Ignacio may contain six hundred whales. Most of the courting and mating takes place near the entrance to the lagoon.

After birthing, the females with calves stay in the upper lagoon for a month or two before the urge hits them to return north to the Arctic feeding grounds.

North for the Summer

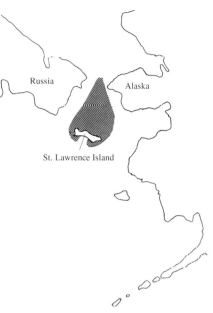

Grays migrate in groups of one to five individuals, and rarely in groups of up to eighteen. Mature whales leave the lagoons first, followed by juveniles. Mothers with calves are the last to leave, often waiting until March. A few stragglers can be found in the lagoons as late as early May.

The northward migration isn't as fast as the southward, for it lacks the birthing urgency of near-term pregnant whales. As it is spread over a four- to six-month period, it is rare to see a hundred whales pass a single point on the coast in one day. A number of whales have been tagged to determine just how fast they migrate. One whale from San Ignacio Lagoon traveled almost 7,000 kilometers (4,620 miles) in ninety-four days, averaging seventy-four kilometers (49 miles) per day. Seventeen other radio-tagged whales averaged 85 kilometers (56 miles) a day, swimming faster toward the end of the long trek, just as my old horse speeds up when he sees the barn. On each of the last twenty-nine days of the migration, the tagged whales averaged 127 kilometers (84 miles) per day. It appears that grays maintain the same approximate speed both day and night, although some time out is taken for rest.

Gray whales do not sleep like humans do, but they do take periods of rest. One biologist estimated that they sleep in half-hour naps about six or seven times a day. Unlike humans, grays do not breathe unconsciously, so in resting they will often float quietly near the surface so that they can rise and breathe. They usually lie with their heads and tails just under the water's surface, with only the arched back showing. Then the head slowly rises, a deep breath is taken, and the whale slowly sinks again. This behavior is called "logging," for the resting whales look just like huge logs bobbing at the water's surface. It is not uncommon for fishing boats to bump into resting whales, giving an unwelcome jolt to both parties.

Although migrating females with calves tend to follow the shoreline more closely, almost all of the migration takes place over the continental shelf, often in water less than nine meters (30 feet) deep. Along the California coast, mothers with calves usually swim in even shallower water within two hundred meters (650 feet) of shore.

Summer feeding grounds of the gray whale.

Resting whales often stay just under the water's surface, in a maneuver known as "logging." (Adrian Dorst)

Gray Whales, *Wandering Giants*

Just how the whales follow the same migration routes year after year is a good question. Memory, the sight of familiar landmarks, and poking their heads above water to get bearings have all been suggested mechanisms. Ray Gilmore, a San Diego-based whale biologist, believes that whales use the remembered taste of sediment in the water off lagoons and estuaries to keep themselves on course.

Part of the navigation may be based on the whales' ability to follow magnetic fields. It is known that finback whales follow magnetic contours rather than cross a geomagnetic gradient, leading some biologists to theorize that magnetic material in the whales' brains allows them to detect magnetic fields. Whether gray whales possess the same material is unknown. Gray whales have anal glands, and some biologists theorize that these glands might excrete a scent that can be detected by other whales. They wonder if grays thus leave some kind of scent trail through the water that grays at the rear of the migration can follow.

Although it used to be believed that gray whales did not feed during migration, this has now been disproved. Anyone who goes to Cow Bay, Cox Bay, Ahous Bay, or Hesquiat Harbour, on the west coast of Vancouver Island, in March is likely to find migrating grays feeding there.

On deep dives, a gray whale's tail flukes are briefly visible at the surface. (Robert H. Busch)

Most migrating grays swim all the way back up the coast to the Bering Sea off Alaska. They pass the Vancouver Island area in March and April. By June, most of the whales stream through Unimak Pass in the eastern Aleutian Islands, which makes it easy for biologists to count the migrating whales. A few weeks later they arrive in the feeding grounds in the Bering Sea, with some continuing on to the Chukchi Sea as far west as Wrangel Island, off the northern coast of Siberia. A few grays head east, enter the Beaufort Sea, and feed in the Mackenzie Delta area.

The Bering and Chukchi feeding grounds are generally shallow, averaging only about fifty to sixty-eight meters (165 to 225 feet) deep. It is estimated that seventy-five percent of the grays feed in the main area located just north of St. Lawrence

The wild west coast of Vancouver Island is the summer home for thirty-five to fifty gray whales. (Robert H. Busch)

Island, between the eastern tip of Russia and the western tip of Alaska. So important are these feeding grounds that Russian biologists recommended in 1982 that they be set aside as a protected area, but so far, no one has acted on this excellent proposal.

Each year some migrating grays never make it to the Arctic feeding grounds. En route, they split off and take up summer residency in various feeding areas. After the summer is over, these whales rejoin the whales migrating south in November. A few grays stay in Baja for the summer and a few stay in the Gulf of Farallon in northern California, just south of the Oregon border. In most years, about thirty grays are resident along the Oregon coast between the mouth of the Alsea River and Cape Foulweather. Others can be found in the Puget Sound area northwest of Seattle. Each year eight or ten grays stray into the Strait of Juan de Fuca and Strait of Georgia. Some even enter the busy Vancouver harbor.

The largest group of summer residents can usually be found off Vancouver Island, where thirty-five to fifty grays regularly stop to spend the summer. Many of these Vancouver Island whales have been given names which are keyed to diagnostic features of their appearance. Two Dot Star, a male who has been summering in the Tofino area for over twenty years, has two prominent white patches on his back. Splotch has a large splotch of white. Ditto is named for the two notches along his back. Prop has scars from an encounter with a boat propeller. Elvis has flippers that are shredded (likely by the teeth of a killer whale), giving him the appearance of Elvis Presley in one of his tackier fringed Las Vegas outfits.

For over twenty years, the resident gray whales of Vancouver Island have been studied by biologist Jim Darling. Although Darling hesitates to say that the whales establish summer home ranges, he says "the whales do show site fidelity, so perhaps foraging routes would be a better term." Most of the residents that come back year after year are mature adults, with relatively few juveniles.

Darling has documented some very unusual resident gray whale behavior:

> *At one point, two whales rolled simultaneously, both showing penes {penises}. These two lay side by side, belly up, with one's penis on the other's underside. Then they intertwined penes for several minutes. Following several more minutes of similar activity all three whales rolled belly up simultaneously and all with semi-erect penes.*

Such behavior, if it resulted in the release of sperm, could be a competitive means of depleting the fertilization capacity of rival males, but the exact reasons for these actions are unknown.

In fact, despite decades of study, much remains to be learned about gray whales. Jim Darling says that the social behavior of gray whales is high on his list of things that we still need to know: "What their mating system is, how they communicate, which is part of social behavior—all of this is still a mystery."

Senses

Hearing

The most important sense to a gray whale is undoubtedly hearing. According to veteran whale biologist Victor B. Scheffer, "every whale everywhere lives in a sea of total sound."

In whales, the auditory nerve is relatively larger than in other mammals, suggesting the importance of hearing. In addition, the lobes of the brain responsible for hearing are highly developed. In the human brain, the centers of sight and hearing are about the same size; in the whale brain, the hearing center is much larger than that of sight.

In water, sound travels four and a half times faster than in air, making it a perfect medium for communication. This was known way back in the days of Aristotle, who once wrote, "Even a small noise ... sounds very heavy and enormous to anything which can hear under water." Sound also travels farther underwater than in air. A twenty-Hz (cycles per second) sound made near the surface of the water could travel over six hundred kilometers (400 miles) under good conditions, so long-distance communication between whales is theoretically quite possible.

Like most cetaceans, gray whales are able to make audible sounds. Both Aristotle and Pliny the Elder wrote about the sounds made by captured dolphins, but their writings seemed to have been forgotten centuries later when fishermen believed that the eerie moans and whistles echoing through their boat hulls came from sea monsters or man-hungry mermaids. It was not until the 1850s that whalers began to report that gray whales make audible sounds that can be heard above the water. In 1889 H.L. Aldrich reported that gray whales "sing" in the Arctic feeding grounds.

We know now that gray whales vocalize through a series of clicks, groans, grunts, squeaks, rasps, and roars. These sounds are produced by squeezing air through the larynx or through the blowhole, or by bursts of air from the lungs. Steven B. Swartz, who studied grays at Baja's San Ignacio Lagoon in the 1970s, says, "There's definitely

FACING PAGE: *In a typical breach, a gray whale rises almost vertically, then falls onto its side.* (Wilfred Atleo)

communication going on amongst them." However, just what they are saying is anybody's guess. Only now are researchers beginning to untangle the whale's repertoire and suggest the meanings of the various sounds.

Researchers in Baja California have noticed that clicks were most often made when a plane or helicopter passed overhead, and wondered if the clicks were an expression of anger or fear. When a captive gray whale held for a short time at Sea World in San Diego was released back into the wild, she emitted a rapid series of clicks that she had never before made in captivity, which may have signaled anger, excitement, fear, or an attempt to communicate with migrating grays. In captivity, her trainer noticed that "when she's happy, there's one big grunt. Her whole body swells up."

University of British Columbia researcher Marilyn Dahlheim taped gray whale vocalizations for two hundred hours at San Ignacio Lagoon in Baja and found a number of situations in which grays were vocal. These situations occurred when grays were grouped in a small area, when they were interacting with bottlenose dolphins, when they were on a collision course with another whale or a boat, when a single whale was chasing a cow and calf, or when boat noise filled the water. She found that the most common sound was a pulsing low-frequency sound between twenty and three thousand Hz. She also confirmed that this sound fell within the frequency range of outboard engine noise, which seems to attract the whales. Researchers in the Chukchi and Bering seas found that even lower frequency whale sounds predominated there, mostly between fourteen and 955 Hz.

Carol Miller, in the San Ignacio Lagoon as part of a research program at Orange Coast College, found that "by rubbing the side of the boat, making it squeak, the whales would surface next to us," suggesting that the grays found the squeaking sound attractive.

In 1966 and 1967, three researchers lowered hydrophones into the water off Point Loma and Point La Jolla, California, to record the sounds of migrating grays. Over thirteen days and nights, they recorded 231 vocalizations comprised

of moans, blowing sounds, and bubble sounds accompanied by a sharp knocking sound. They found that the whales were vocal both night and day.

Recognizing the importance of hearing to gray whales, some people have tried serenading the animals with human sounds. Researcher Jim Nollman used a whale singer, made from Native American drums, to play for whales off the coast of California. In Baja, Paul Winter and seventy other musicians sat on an island in Bahia Magdalena and played to the wintering whales. In neither case did the musicians receive a round of applause from their audience, in part because the sounds they were playing were too high frequency for the gray whales to hear.

Unlike dolphins and killer whales, gray whales do not appear to use high frequency sounds for echo-location. Researcher Ken Norris once strung a series of aluminum poles across a channel in San Ignacio Lagoon to test the grays' ability to echo-locate submerged items. The bottle-nosed dolphins in the lagoon easily detected and evaded the poles, but a mother gray whale and her calf never detected them, crashing into them once and then again in a panic to escape.

FACING PAGE: *The gray whale's eye is about the size of an orange.* (François Gohier)

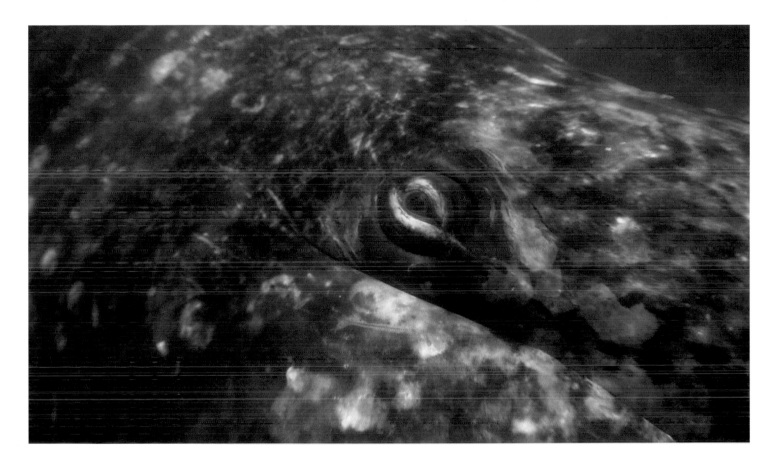

Sight

Because the eyes of the gray whale are located so far back on its head, it does not possess good binocular vision like humans do. Its field of vision consists mainly of two monocular fields on both sides of its body; items located just in front of its nose cannot be seen at all.

There is some question just how good the eyesight of a whale is; physically, their eyes are quite small. Human eyes make up about one-seventieth of our body mass; whale eyes are only about one-six-hundredth of their total mass. Although the eye and optic nerve are rather undeveloped in gray whales, they seem to have fair eyesight in both water and air.

The gray whale's eyeball is a nearly spherical lens. At the back of the eye is a layer of cells called the tapetum, which acts like a mirror to reflect light back to the retina over and over again, a great aid in low light conditions such as murky water. The retina also contains a large number of rod cells, which are sensitive to low light. It has a smaller number of cone cells, which give sharpness to the image, suggesting that much of what is seen is rather blurry. Despite this handicap, a young gray whale kept in captivity for a short while at Sea World in San Diego could recognize her trainer on sight, even when his features were almost completely hidden in a wetsuit.

Other observers have also noted that gray whales appear to see quite well in air. Rod Palm, a whale researcher on Vancouver Island, once found a young gray in very shallow water close to a beach. When he walked along the beach, the whale followed in the water. When he changed direction, the whale changed too. Finally the curious whale drove itself up onto the sand, took a close look at Palm, and then slid back into the water.

Gray whales are frequently spotted "spy-hopping," a maneuver in which they poke their heads straight up out of the water to look around. It was once thought that they stood on their tails on the ocean bottom in order to do this, but grays have been seen spy-hopping in very deep water and obviously can spy-hop merely by treading water with their tail flukes.

It is not known what degree of color vision is possessed by gray whales. All that we have are bits of anecdotal evidence, such as what happened in 1988 when three grays were trapped in Arctic ice in Alaska (see page 112). Arnold Brower Jr., who acted as a field staffer for the National Oceanic and Atmospheric Administration, reported having to chase away reporters who wore red. "Upon noticing that kind of color," he said, "the whales dive whether they have taken enough breath or not."

*This gray whale calf in San Ignacio
Lagoon is doing a very high spy-hop.*
(Frank S. Balthis/Nature's Design)

Smell

The anatomy of their brains shows that the sense of smell is very poorly developed in whales. In addition, baleen whales like the gray whale have only a small patch of smell receptors in their nasal passages. Smell plays a very small role in their watery world.

Touch

Contrary to the beliefs of early whalers, many whales have a relatively well-developed sense of touch, and their epidermis is quite thin. We can only imagine the horrible pain they once felt when whaling harpoons pierced their flesh.

Gray whales are certainly able to detect when their blowholes are above the water's surface, and many a whale-watcher has been surprised when a gray whale responds to the touch of a human hand with what looks like a shiver. Female grays and their young frequently touch each other with what humans would call caresses, and although the digits in the flippers cannot be moved individually, the entire flipper is often used to fondle a mate or newborn calf. The increasing number of grays that like to rub against rubber boats or dinghies also suggests that whale skin may be richer in nerve endings than we once thought. In addition, many grays each year linger in the kelp beds off California to roll and slide through the kelp, suggesting that the feel is quite pleasurable.

Taste

The ability of the gray whale to detect different flavors is a matter of some debate. Since grays do not chew their food, but swallow it whole, it would follow that they do not need a well-developed sense of taste.

Although there are taste buds at the base of their tongues, the nerves leading to the area are very small in size and number. Some biologists believe that the gray whale just sucks in whatever food it can and is unable to discern favorite flavors or

FACING PAGE: *The baleen plates of a gray whale are fringed at the bottom to strain out food items.* (Bob Cranston)

tastes. Others believe that a rudimentary sense of taste must exist in order for the whale to select out favorite food items. Gigi, a young gray kept at Sea World in San Diego in the 1970s, was given nine kilograms (30 pounds) of squid at a time, but if a few mackerel were thrown in, she would consistently spit out the mackerel.

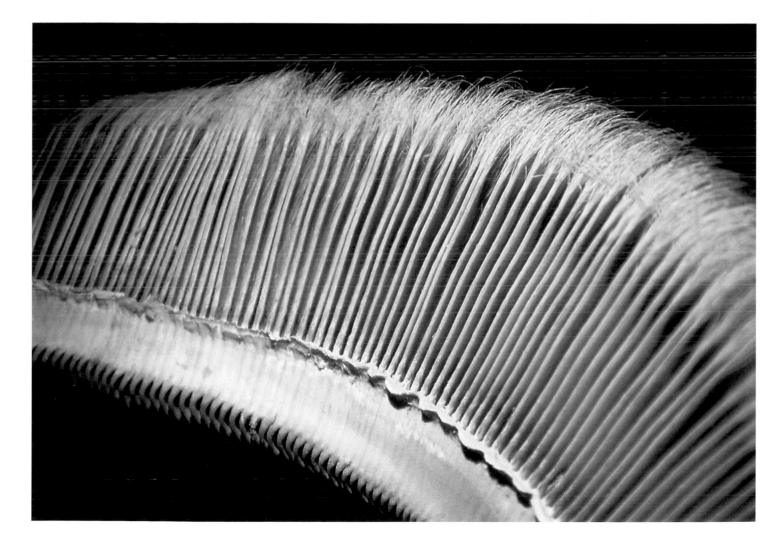

Swimming and Diving

Gray whales swim with a lazy-looking up-and-down motion of their huge horizontal tail flukes. It has been estimated that this motion is the equivalent of a five hundred-horsepower engine mounted at the rear of the whale. So efficient is the movement that it looks quite effortless. Philippe Cousteau once described the motion as "incomparably supple … not separate motions, but one beautifully coordinated action." The movement of the tail is accomplished by a massive muscle system. In fact, the muscle system of the gray whale accounts for a third of its total body weight.

The excellent streamlining of the whale's body reduces drag in the water, and the whale's epidermis excretes tiny droplets of oil that decrease drag even further. In addition, the outer layer of skin is shed rapidly, and this sloughing skin helps to reduce drag. Whales in captivity sometimes must be brushed down to remove this skin to prevent the body surface from becoming gummy and infected.

Whales are made buoyant through a specialized bone structure and through a thick layer of blubber. The hard outer bone covers a spongy web-like inner structure which is laced with blood vessels. The gaps between the tissues and vessels are filled with a marrow high in oil content, and since oil is lighter than water, some whale bones actually can float on water. In addition, a thick layer of blubber rich in oil provides buoyancy. The long, narrow body of the gray whale allows it to maneuver in water less than three meters (10 feet) deep, much shallower than the limit for other whales.

The normal cruising speed for a gray whale is from three to nine kilometers (2 to 6 miles) per hour, although bursts of speed at twice that rate may result when fleeing predators.

Biologist Ray Gilmore described a special type of swimming which he calls "evasive swimming," in which grays swim just below the surface, exposing only the blowhole, and exhaling slowly before sinking and swimming away. Gilmore believed that this is a defensive maneuver used to evade predators.

Normally, a gray whale will surface and breathe two or three times at ten- to

FACING PAGE: *The dual blowholes of the gray whale close tightly before a deep dive.* (Richard Beaupied/The Whale Centre, Tofino, BC)

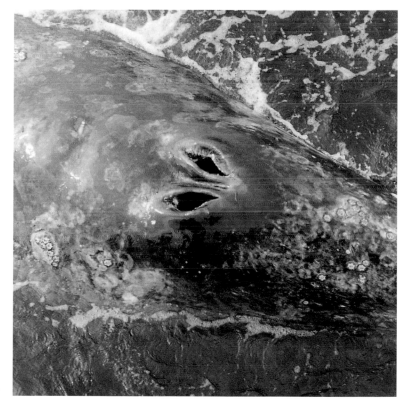

twenty-second intervals before submerging for three to five minutes. Unlike seals, which exhale before diving, whales, like humans, take a deep breath first. Grays usually take only shallow dives, reappearing about three hundred meters (1,000 feet) from the spot at which they dove.

For deep dives, a gray whale may take two or three breaths every minute for three to five minutes, and then plunge into the ocean. On deep dives, the whale's tail flukes may be visible above the water for quite a while, to the delight of nature photographers and whale-watchers. The whale may stay under water for up to twenty-five minutes and not reappear at the surface until it is 800 meters (2,600 feet) away.

When a gray whale sinks beneath the surface, it leaves a broad oval patch of calm water at the surface, known as a "footprint," the result of water upwelling from the whale's tail flukes. Sometimes this mark is the only clue that a huge whale lurks below.

Most gray whale dives are to less than thirty meters (100 feet), but it is thought that they can dive to a maximum of about 120 meters (395 feet). (A humpback whale, which also is usually a shallow diver, was once found entangled in submarine cable at 119 meters [390 feet].) Very few of the gray's food items live at these depths, so there is really no reason for it to go any deeper.

During a deep dive, the valves around the whale's blowhole close tightly to keep out water. Whales also have a couple of adaptations which allow them to dive deeply without damage. The sclera, the white part of the whale's eye, is thick and resilient and can take high pressures without deforming. In addition, a whale's rib cage is quite flexible, unlike a human's, and bends easily under pressure without breaking.

The dual blowholes of the gray whale produce a heart-shaped blow in calm wind conditions. (Jamie Bray/Jamie's Whaling Station, Tofino, BC)

Upon surfacing, the first breath of exhaled air often results in a blow or spout that may be three meters (10 feet) high. In calm weather, the blow can be seen to be heart-shaped, due to the dual blowholes of the gray whale. In a single big blow, almost 378 liters (100 gallons) of air may be expelled. If a breath is exhaled slowly, the blow is hardly visible at all.

The blow or spout of a whale appears misty, primarily due to the condensation of warm expelled air—the same reason that steam swirls above a hot cup of coffee—but part of it may be due to tiny oil droplets. An oily foam is present in the breathing passages and this oil may mix with expelled air to produce a visible mist. A small part of the mist may also result from water that remains in the shallow depression around the whale's blowhole, which is atomized into mist when it blows.

The spouts of a whale were long thought to be poisonous. Herman Melville, author of *Moby Dick*, wrote in 1851: "If the jet is fairly spouted into your eyes, it will blind you."

In actual fact, it is not poisonous at all, but it occasionally does have a powerful smell. John Steinbeck wrote in *The Log from the Sea of Cortez*: "A whale's breath is frightfully sickening. It smells of complete decay." To another writer, the expelled air smelled like a day-old can of tuna-flavored cat food. However, all of the whale spouts I have smelled have had no odor at all, so perhaps the smell only develops when the whale is ill, diseased, or wounded, or after it has just fed.

Breaching

One of the most awesome sights in the animal kingdom is that of a great whale soaring up out of the water and crashing back, a maneuver that is known as breaching.

Although humpback and killer whales appear to breach more often than grays, gray whales do breach quite regularly. In a typical breach, a whale will swim underwater very rapidly and then suddenly raise its head up, turning the horizontal speed into a vertical force that sends it up out of the water. It then usually turns and lands on its side or back with a tremendous splash. Often a gray whale will breach two or three times in a row; Lyall Watson, in his *Sea Guide to Whales of the World*, reported "thirty-eight consecutive leaps in a manic sequence by a large male."

Breaching gray whales were described by Captain Charles Scammon in the late 1800s, so breaching is not something new. But what is the reason for such a bizarre action? Certainly many breaches are just part of play or burning off energy, the whale's equivalent of my horse's kicking up his heels and prancing around his field. Some studies have found that juveniles breach more often than adults, suggesting that juvenile play is at work.

Other observers have found that adult males breach more often than females. This suggests that breaching may be part of courtship, of intimidating other males or showing off for females in order to woo a mate. Biologists report that breaching does occur more often in the winter, the season of courtship and mating, than in the summer, which might strengthen this suggestion. And social breeds of whale tend to breach more often than whales which do not have much organized social behavior.

Observers in Alaska once noticed that humpback whales breached repeatedly when

This gray whale delighted dockside crowds in Tofino, BC, in 1988 with its repeated breaches.
(Richard Beaupied/The Whale Centre, Tofino, BC)

a cruise ship passed by, each breach following a spurt of noise from the ship's huge engines. But just what was the engine noise saying in whale language? Whale biologist Hal Whitehead believes that breaching may be a way to emphasize a visual or auditory signal among whales. Just as people raise their voices to make a point, whales may breach to do the same thing. Biologist Roger Payne believes that breaching increases as wind increases, as it helps whales communicate when wave noise would drown out normal vocalizations.

Other biologists have found that the airborne sound of a breaching whale falling back on the water can travel as far as six kilometers (4 miles) under good conditions, and have speculated whether the sound is some sort of communication signal among whales. The underwater sound produced, though, is very small.

Biologist Ted Walker, and others, think that breaching is sometimes used to make emergency course corrections. Walker once watched a migrating gray whale that was on a collision course with a pier near La Jolla, California. He described what happened in the March 1971 issue of *National Geographic*:

> At the last moment the whale burst from the sea at a 45-degree angle.
> Then it breached again and again, each time falling back on its side
> and heading a few more degrees toward the open sea. By the time the
> whale had made ten lunges out of the sea, it was clear of the obstacle
> and back on course.

Breaching may also be a way for gray whales to knock off pesky lice and barnacles. Lacking the use of movable hands, a whale might use a giant crash back into the waves to loosen and dislodge its heavy parasite load.

Breaching is definitely a form of whale behavior that delights nature photographers. Richard Beaupied, owner of The Whale Centre in Tofino, British Columbia, has an excellent photo of a breaching gray whale on the wall of his museum. The photo clearly shows the two giant flippers of the whale as it soars into the air and lands on its back. He says that a tourist once took a good look at the photo and exclaimed with a straight face, "My, what big ears those whales have!"

Breathing

If a human tried to dive to the depths that whales do, his breath would soon run out and he would have to scramble back to the surface. Just how does a whale perform the same feat? The answer comes from a series of adaptations that make whales much more efficient at breathing than humans.

For one thing, a whale's muscle tissue is high in myoglobin, an iron-based protein similar to the hemoglobin in human blood. Myoglobin stores oxygen and allows whales to dive for extended periods of time without taking another breath. The massive myoglobin-rich muscle system of whales actually acts as a big oxygen storehouse; whales store forty-one percent of their oxygen in their muscles, compared to the thirteen percent that humans can store. In addition, whales have up to two or three times more blood per unit of body weight than humans, further enabling them to store oxygen. The gray whale's heart alone weighs over 130 kilograms (285 pounds). Third, a whale's lungs have more alveoli, or air cells, than ours, and two layers of capillaries (opposed to our one), greatly increasing the efficiency of air exchange. Most whales' lungs can remove about twice as much oxygen from air as human lungs. Gray whales breathe at about thirty to fifty breaths per hour, and their lungs are much bigger than hu-

When a gray whale feeds on the ocean bottom, sometimes all that shows at the surface is one half of the huge tail flukes, often mistaken for a dorsal fin. (Robert H. Busch)

The huge tongue of a gray whale is revealed in this beached specimen. (Richard Beaupied/The Whale Centre, Tofino, BC)

mans', averaging about 300 kilograms (730 pounds).

Each massive whale breath expels about eighty to ninety percent of the intaken air. Humans expel about fifteen percent, so whales are about five or six times more efficient at getting rid of the oxygen-depleted air that they have breathed in and used.

When they dive, whales take a series of rapid breaths which saturate their pulmonary system with oxygen, just as human swimmers hyperventilate before beginning a race. On a deep dive, a whale's heart rate slows down and the blood flow is restricted, so the oxygen supply is depleted very slowly. This adaptation is known as brachycardia. The heart rate often decreases from a normal eight to ten beats per minute to half that, only four to five beats per minute. This decreased rate is about a tenth the rate required by a human diver. Upon resurfacing, the whale's heart rate returns to its normal rate and blood flow resumes its former rate.

Human divers have to worry about getting the "bends," a painful malady in which nitrogen and other gases form bubbles in the blood if the diver comes to the surface too fast. Whales have no such worries, for their blubber absorbs some of the nitrogen and the rest is trapped by the foamy oil in the nasal sacs and sinuses. The nitrogen is then expelled with this oil when the whale spouts.

All in all, the whale is a swimming and diving machine, perfectly adapted for its life in the water.

Keeping Warm

The gray whale's normal internal temperature is about 37 to 38°C (96 to 99°F). But at the northern end of the gray whale's migration, they often swim in water that is only 3 to 4°C (37 to 39°F), so how do they prevent their bodies from losing valuable heat?

First, the gray whale is insulated from the cold outside water by five inches of excellent insulation in the form of blubber. Contrary to popular myth, whale blubber is not pure fat, but a complex mix of fibrous, fatty, and connective tissues that is honeycombed with large oil-filled cells. The thickest layers of blubber are found in pregnant females, which have precious fetuses to protect.

Blubber is incredibly effective at keeping whales warm, and even after death, the rate of cooling is very slow. Scientists once put a thermometer in a dead finback whale and were surprised to find twenty-eight hours later that the muscle temperature had dropped only 1.5 degrees. In fact, dead whales often explode from the trapped internal heat combined with the heat generated by decomposition, and exploding carcasses were part of the risks taken by early whalers.

The second adaptation for low heat loss is that whales are blessed with a low ratio of surface area to body volume, giving them a relatively small area that is available to heat loss.

Another adaptation lies in their circulatory system. A gray whale's arteries and veins lie side by side, so cooled blood from the surface is warmed before it goes to the heart.

And finally, one way to keep warm is to eat. Protein yields more warmth per pound than other foods, and the gray whale's diet is almost nothing but protein-rich seafood.

Feeding Behavior

Gray whales feed upon a variety of different foods in a variety of different ways. Primarily, they are bottom feeders. This was recognized as early as 1865 by Captain Charles Scammon, who wrote of a gray's "head and lips besmeared with the dark ooze from the depths below."

In order to feed off the bottom of the ocean, a gray whale will swim down to the bottom, roll onto its side, and plunge its head a few inches into the muck. By expanding and contracting its throat grooves, and retracting its huge tongue (which may weigh 1,300 kilograms [3,000 pounds]), suction is created that sucks the bottom mud into the whale's mouth. There the food is moved around a bit by the tongue and then pushed out through the baleen, the horny plates which hang down from the whale's upper jaw like a big curtain. The food items are trapped by the baleen and the rest is pushed out the sides of the mouth. The whale then swallows the mouthful of goodies and goes back for more.

That's the basic process, but the details are quite fascinating. Firstly, it appears that gray whales are "right-handed." From the wear of the barnacles on the right side of the head and degree of wear on the baleen plates on the right side of the mouth, biologists deduce that most gray whales use the right side of their mouths for sucking in food.

The action of the baleen plates is also interesting. The gray whale has about 160 pairs of baleen plates which hang down on both sides of the upper jaw. Each plate is a grayish-yellow color, up to thirty-eight centimeters (15 inches) long and up to twenty-five centimeters (10 inches) wide. The plates are made of keratin, the same stuff that makes up human fingernails. The top of each plate, where it is anchored in the jaw, is hard and solid, but the leading edge of the plate is feathered into hard bristles rather like a toothbrush. The question is how these bristles screen out food and reject the rest. And the answer is sometimes they don't.

Although grays are able to spit out food items that do not appeal to them, often they ingest by accident items that are totally inedible, and their stomach contents often include sand and pebbles. Sometimes a gray whale will make two passes through

The food items of the gray whale are incredibly small. (Frank S. Balthis/ Nature's Design)

the muds, the first just to stir up the top inch or so, and the second to gulp in the resulting cloud of floating organisms. In this way, grays can avoid to some degree the heavier sand grains and other inedibles.

Although gray whales are quite capable of swallowing while in a horizontal position, some biologists think that in deep water, grays will assume a vertical, head-up position to help the food slide down. Veteran whale biologist Ted Walker even thinks that some of the spy-hopping he has seen can be explained as a swallowing maneuver, as the whales have their eyes closed at the time and so are obviously not looking around.

A gray whale feeds by plunging the right side of its mouth into the ocean bottom. (Bob Cranston)

Grice Bay is a favorite feeding area for summer resident grays in BC's Pacific Rim National Park. (Robert H. Busch)

As you can imagine, by the time an animal the size of a whale finishes bottom feeding in an area, it looks like a minefield. In Grice Bay, near Tofino on Vancouver Island, you can walk out at low tide and see the huge pits in the bottom mud left by the grays. The pits, up to three meters (10 feet) long, remind me of huge divots, as if some giant bad golfer had played nine holes through the bay. In the Bering Sea, where the grays feed in the summer, it is estimated that a minimum of 171 tonnes (156 tons) of bottom sediment is sifted by gray whales each year.

By plowing through the bottom muds, gray whales stir up nutrients which feed a long list of other marine creatures. The plume of mud that results from a gray whale that is bottom feeding streams behind it like a giant feather and is a good clue to what is going on below.

But just what do gray whales feed upon in the bottom muds? The answer to that includes a long list of amphipods, isopods, gastropods, bivalve molluscs, hydrozoans, and worms. Probably the most important of these are the amphipods. Amphipods are tiny crustaceans that look like little shrimp. There are over 4,600 amphipod species, which range from tiny things about the size of the period at the end of this sentence to big beasts over two centimeters (1 inch) long. In many surveys, amphipods make up as much as ninety percent of the gray whale's diet. In the Arctic feeding grounds, the six-millimeter- (quarter-inch-) long species *Ampelisca macrocephala* is a popular gray whale food item.

In Grice Bay, the big attraction is the ghost shrimp (*Caprella linearis*). Biologists have found that the gray whales in Grice Bay are restricted by their size to how far up the beach they can feed. But ghost shrimp live right up to the intertidal zone, which means that Mother Nature has once again ensured that some shrimp will always escape the feeding gray whales and live on to reproduce the species.

Another kind of shrimp known as mysid shrimp or opposum shrimp are favorite food items, especially the species *Holmesimysis sculpta* and *Neomysis rayii*, which can be found in large swarms just above the bottom. Grays have been observed feeding along the crevices of bottom rocks which act as natural sluices for mysids. They will even push around big boulders weighing hundreds of pounds to get at this tasty type of seafood. Bottom mats of the tube-dwelling worm *Diopatra* are also a popular food among gray whales.

But gray whales are not just bottom feeders. They also feed upon floating and swimming organisms. Often they lie on their right sides at the ocean's surface, slowly gulping in mouthfuls of nutrient-filled water, again showing their preference for "right-handedness." In San Ignacio Lagoon, gray whales will place themselves where the currents are the strongest, and lie there with mouths open, letting the waves wash food in.

In the Arctic, grays scoop up vast swarms of floating plankton. Further south, they have been seen circling tightly, apparently feeding on spawning squid. Grays have also been seen swimming at the surface with their mouths open, gulping in schools of anchovies and other small fish. In the spring, they often dine on swarms of krill, the common name for euphasiid shrimp.

In Hesquiat Harbour on the west coast of Vancouver Island, hundreds of grays gather each year to dine on herring roe. For two or three weeks the grays feed on floating roe, and when the roe in the shallow bay is depleted, the whales leave the bay and continue on their trek north.

In the spring, grays may also dine on the larvae of crabs which float at the water's surface. On the

The right side of this gray whale's head has numerous scars, probably caused by bottom feeding.
(Wilfred Atleo)

This gray whale feeding north of St. Lawrence Island in the Bering Sea has stirred up a prominent mud plume. (Howard Braham/ National Marine Mammal Laboratory)

west coast of Vancouver Island, grays gather every spring in Cow Bay to feed on thick clouds of crab larvae. Later in the crab life cycle, in May or June when they are tiny bottom-dwellers, they become part of the grays' ocean-bottom menu. And on the Baja coast, grays feed on dense shoals of tiny red crabs (*Pleuroncodes planipes*).

Gray whales also will scrape small crustaceans off kelp and eelgrass. Biologist Mary Lou Jones once watched in awe as a gray whale in Baja's San Ignacio Lagoon fed on eelgrass. "It was sucking them down, one by one, just like a gopher pulling turnips underground," she says. Sometimes it appears that grays actually swallow the kelp or eelgrass itself. A diver in San Diego once photographed a gray whale eating kelp and defecating the round floats that are part of the plant. A gray whale found stranded at Wauna, Washington, was found to have ninety-eight liters (26 gallons) of kelp and algae in its stomach. Captain Charles Scammon reported in 1874 that most of the gray whales taken in the Baja lagoons had "sea moss" in their stomachs, which presumably means eelgrass. It is likely that grays use these plants to scour out intestinal upsets, just as dogs occasionally eat grass for the same purpose.

While in the Arctic over the summer, it is estimated that a gray whale will eat about seventy-three tonnes (67 tons) of food, or about four hundred kilograms (900 pounds) per day. Other estimates of the daily intake range up to 1,360 kilograms (3,000 pounds) of food per day. A yearling gray whale kept for a short time at Sea World in San Diego ate over eight hundred kilograms (1,800 pounds) of squid every day. On the average it is thought that a mature gray whale will devour about a ton of food every day.

Although that sounds like a lot of food, gray whales are actually very efficient feeders. Their metabolic rate is very low, so they make efficient use of food energy. A human burns about seventy-five kilocalories of food per day per pound of body weight, but a gray whale burns only about seven. It thus is about ten times as efficient an eater as we are, yet another example of how perfectly and efficiently it has evolved.

Intelligence

The brain of a gray whale bears a striking resemblance to the human brain, but the intelligence of a whale is a difficult subject to quantify. Just how do you measure intelligence? Sure, you can put together intelligence tests for humans, but how do you put together tests for whales, or chimps, or insects? As Doc once said in John Steinbeck's *Cannery Row*, "We can only use ourselves as a yardstick," and perhaps that's not a very good measure.

Two rough indices of intelligence used in the past have been the degree of brain convolution and brain volume. The cerebral cortex of a whale's brain is indeed covered with convolutions and fissures, which in humans is the sign of a well-developed centralized nervous system. But so far no one has been able to directly equate convolutions with intelligence.

Brain volume is also a dubious standard. Fully twenty percent of the gray whale's brain bulk by weight is due to the cerebellum, which controls voluntary movement and balance. This is the reason for the gray whale's great ability to maneuver in very shallow water. Relative to their brain size, the cerebellum of a whale is over fifty percent larger than that of a human, which explains our general clumsiness—we are smart, but we're not too graceful.

Whale brains have well-developed frontal lobes, which are the seat of conceptual intelligence in humans, but there again the degree of development is difficult to quantify. Harry J. Jerison at the University of California, Los Angeles, once developed a concept he called "encephalization quotient," or EQ. In Jerison's system, he compared the brain size to the body weight of the animal, giving an animal with an average-sized brain for its body weight the value of 1.0. Animals with relatively smaller brains received a value less than 1.0 and animals with larger than average-sized brains received a value of more than 1.0. On Jerison's list, the animal with the highest EQ was the human. The small toothed whales placed high on the list, but baleen whales generally received EQs less than 1.0.

It is generally accepted that toothed whales biologically should have a higher intelligence than baleen whales, for the former have to chase and outwit prey, while the latter don't need a lot of brains to suck up vast clouds of plankton, krill, and small crustaceans.

Other biologists have expressed brain weight as a percentage of body weight and used this as a rough guide to intelligence. The human brain makes up almost two percent of the human body's total weight. The brains of dolphins and chimpanzees weigh in at about 0.75 percent, still a respectable number. Of the large whales, the species with the largest brain is the sperm whale, with a huge ten-kilogram (22-pound) brain that makes up only .025 percent of its total body weight. Gray whales come even lower on the list, with 4.3-kilogram (9.5-pound) brains that make up only about .01 percent of their total body weight.

Yet when you think of it, is EQ or percentage brain weight really a good measure of intelligence? Einstein's brain was only average-sized relative to the brains of other humans, but no one could ever say that he had only average intelligence. So perhaps the best answer to the intelligence question is that gray whales are probably less intelligent than the small toothed whales and certainly less intelligent than humans. But they are as intelligent as they need to be for their survival, and that is all that really counts.

The back of a gray whale has a series of low bumps known as knuckles. (Wilfred Atleo)

Social Behavior

Whale biologist Kenneth Balcomb once noted, "We literally know more about the solar system than we know about the social dynamics of whales." His statement is especially true when it is applied to gray whales.

A spy-hopping gray taking a good look at tourists on the west coast of Vancouver Island.
(Wilfred Atleo)

Biologist Jim Darling has studied gray whales for over twenty years, but the social behavior of whales is still on the top of his list of things to learn about grays. "Most books just say that the only gray whale social unit is the mother and calf, but I suspect it is a lot more complex than that," he says. But observations on the social behavior of gray whales are lacking and the topic is a difficult one for which to find funding. All we have for now are a few tantalizing tidbits of information that suggest that the gray whale social organization is more complex than we once thought.

For example, early whalers believed that adult gray whale males would come to the rescue of females, but that the reverse would never happen. Biologists scoffed at such notions for many years, but in the 1950s Russian biologist B.A. Zenkovich reported observing two adult male gray whales supporting an injured female in shallow water.

In 1968, Jacques Cousteau and his team of divers spent some time in the Baja breeding lagoons, watching and filming the gray whales gathered there. Jacques' son Philippe watched one very interesting example of social behavior and was astute enough to write it down:

As soon as they sensed they were being followed, the gray whales all sounded at the same time. But while the group made a ninety-degree turn, a lone whale surfaced in front of the boat and continued swimming for quite some distance in the original direction.

He believed that the whale was offering itself as a decoy, and suggested that this required "an extraordinary degree of understanding among members of the group." On another occasion, "the decoy whale made a great show of diving and then reappearing to the rear of [the boat], hoping no doubt to throw us even further off the track of the group."

Jacques Cousteau also noted some interesting social behavior that involved a second female acting as a "guardian aunt" to a new calf: "When we tried to maneuver in such a way as to isolate the young whale, one of the two whales always succeeded in getting between our Zodiac and the calf." He went on to describe the actions of the "aunt" whale: "One of the two females kept spouting, turning, and seemed very excited." Cousteau and his crew followed this female, then looked around and discovered that the mother and calf had disappeared. "The whole thing had been a trick to get us away from the calf," he concluded.

On the west coast of Vancouver Island, Jim Darling has become "used to seeing certain [gray] whales together." For example, two grays known as Saddle and Whitepatch are "usually, but not always, together." Are they brother and sister? Or just good friends? No one yet knows, but as Darling says, "their relationship also could be a hint at a level of social organization in gray whales below the overall herd structure."

Two juvenile resident gray whales take time out to play off the west coast of Vancouver Island.
(Wilfred Atleo)

What are we to make of these observations, or of the observations by Swartz and Jones of two females helping a stranded calf off a sand bar, or of the groups of mothers and calves that associate in the nursery lagoons? To many biologists, the gray whale is a docile, quiet animal that doesn't attract much interest. One Canadian killer whale biologist recently bluntly described the gray as "boring." But perhaps it only seems that way because we know so little about its social behavior. The glimpses of its social organization that we do have suggest that the gray whale is far from boring; it is only our own ignorance that has gotten in the way.

The explanation behind apparent homosexual activity among young resident male gray whales is unknown. (Wilfred Atleo)

Relationships With Other Species

According to most reports, gray whales get along peacefully with most other marine species, with the obvious exception of their predators.

Russian biologist Alexey Yablokov has reported that "gray whales coexist peacefully with the other mammals inhabiting the Chukchi Sea." He has noted that "near the largest hauling ground of the walrus on Arakamchechen Island, whales and walrus graze in very close proximity to each other. Observers have never recorded any aggressive behavior between these two species." Humpback whales also inhabit the same Arctic feeding grounds, and the two types of whales seem to get along fine.

A gray whale watching the Steller's sea lions at Carmanah Point on the west coast of Vancouver Island. (Rod Palm)

Along the coast of British Columbia, gray whales and Steller's sea lions are often found in the same waters. Grays are sometimes seen spy-hopping watching the antics of their smaller cousins with apparent interest, but no animosity. Whale researcher Rod Palm has even seen a sea lion grabbing a quick ride on the back of a gray whale, although the whale concerned quickly dove to rid itself of the unwanted hitchhiker. Another sea mammal, the rightwhale dolphin, has been observed riding the bow waves of gray whales, taking advantage of the opportunity for a bit of surfing.

Many types of sea birds will also land on gray whales' backs for a quick perch, apparently attracted by the food items stirred up by the whales' feeding. Again, no-one has ever seen a gray act aggressively toward the birds, further evidence of its calm and cool attitude.

Predation, Diseases, and Longevity

Although large sharks such as hammerheads, great white sharks, and tiger sharks occasionally are able to grab a young gray whale calf, the most serious natural predator of gray whales is the killer whale, or orca (*Orcinus orca*).

Killer whales are the main predators of gray whales. (Robert H. Busch)

Along much of the western coast of North America, orcas are divided into two groups: residents and transients. Resident orcas feed primarily on fish. Transient orcas feed on seals, porpoises, otters, and occasionally on small whales. As the late whale biologist Michael Bigg once said, "It's as though the two had agreed on some sort of treaty: 'I'll eat one kind of food, you eat another.' This way they can stay in the same area and not compete." (Recently, a third group has been discovered that has been dubbed offshore orcas. It is not yet known if these are a combination of residents and transients or a different race altogether.)

In one study of gray whales at a California whaling station in the 1960s, an amazing eighteen percent of the carcasses showed evidence of an orca attack. Many gray whales today bear scars along their flippers or tail flukes which match the tooth spacing of orcas. In 1968, Jacques Cousteau and his team of divers saw "killer whales lying in ambush just at the entry of the [Matancitas] lagoon" in Baja, as well as four-meter (13-foot) great white sharks, although they never witnessed an actual attack. In 1971, biologist William C. Cummings and psychologist Paul O. Thompson reported that they had played killer whale sounds via underwater speakers to migrating gray whales and the grays noticeably veered away from the sounds.

Killer whales attacking Greenland whale. (Dover Pictorial Archive)

There have been relatively few eyewitness accounts of orca attacks on gray whales, most of which have been upon small whale calves. Each is worth recounting, as they provide an unusual look at killer whale feeding habits. As early as 1874, Captain Charles Scammon recorded an incident in Baja California in which three orcas attacked a gray whale cow and calf, killing and eating the latter. He likened the orca attack to:

> *a pack of hounds holding the stricken deer at bay. They cluster about*
> *the animal's head, some of their number breaching over it, while others*
> *seize it by the lips and haul the bleeding monster underwater; and*
> *when {it is} captured ... they eat out its tongue.*

Occasionally, a gray whale under attack from orcas will seem to give up, floating belly up as if it were offering itself to the orca. In 1911, naturalist Roy Chapman Andrews witnessed one such attack when he was aboard a Japanese whaler off the Korean coast:

Utterly disregarding our ship, the killers made straight for the gray whale. The beast, twice the size of the killers, seemed paralyzed with fright. Instead of trying to get away, it turned belly up, flippers outspread, awaiting its fate. A killer came at full speed, forced its head into the whale's mouth and ripped out great hunks of soft, spongy tongue. Other killers were tearing at the throat and belly while the poor creature rolled in agony. I was glad when a harpoon ended its torture.

Andrews also reported in 1914 of gray whales retreating into shallow water and trying to hide behind rocks when approached by orcas.

In 1954, Russian biologist B.A. Zenkovich found the tongue and baleen plates of a gray whale in the stomach of an orca taken in the western Bering Sea, proof of a successful attack. Alan Baldridge of Stanford University's Hopkins Marine Station

Many gray whale tails show scars and bites from killer whales. (Wilfred Atleo)

watched five or six orcas stalk a gray whale cow and calf in 1967. The orcas killed the calf, eating its tongue, and stripping blubber off its belly. Teeth marks on the calf's flukes and flippers suggested that the orcas had "restrained and drowned their prey." In another 1967 incident, a mother and calf accompanied by another gray whale all headed into the rough surf zone and escaped attack by a group of orcas.

In the late 1970s, biologists Mary Lou Jones and Steve Swartz watched an orca attack and kill a gray whale calf in San Ignacio Lagoon. They also witnessed five killer whales attack a mother gray whale and calf off the Channel Islands in southern California and recounted their story in Jim Darling's book *With the Whales*:

The killer whales were like a swarm of gnats or bees going in all directions—under, around and in between the female and calf. As we circled, we watched the killer whales separate the mother from her calf. The mother was just going bananas, swinging her head and hitting the killer whales on a couple of occasions. She also hit them with her flukes. In the meantime the calf just disappeared ... They must have drowned it ... The mother was just left on the surface, often doubling back on her track. It appeared to us that she was searching ... She looked exhausted and beat.

In 1987, a twelve-meter (39-foot) adult male gray whale washed up on the rocks below Pachena Lighthouse on the west coast of Vancouver Island. The carcass had seven huge chunks bitten out of its flanks, the gory result of an orca attack.

Biologist Virgil Hawkes witnessed an attack in 1990 by five transient orcas on a lone gray whale feeding in Barkley Sound on the west coast of Vancouver Island. The orcas attacked the head area of the whale, badly injuring it, and then departed. Finally it became too dark to see, and Hawkes was unable to see the outcome of the attack.

Another attack was documented by biologists in 1991 off the California coast. The attack was even captured on videotape, only the second time that a whale-on-whale attack had ever been filmed. A group of about ten orcas followed a female gray and calf and finally forced the calf away from the mother's side. Two of the orcas pulled at the calf's flippers, while another repeatedly struck at the calf with its tail flukes. By the time one researcher arrived at the scene, all that remained were large chunks of blubber floating on the water's surface, in water tainted crimson with blood.

In May 1992, two biologists, P. Dawn Goley and Janice M. Straley, witnessed an attack by at least seventeen orcas on a gray whale mother and calf off Monterey Bay, California. Groups of four or more orcas harassed the pair for five to ten minutes, then were replaced by another group, in a well-coordinated team effort. The orcas struck at the female with their heads, their flanks, and their tail flukes. Blood streaming from the calf's mouth showed that it too had been attacked. When the pair of whales tried to swim away, five orcas "positioned themselves in front of the gray whales in a crescent formation, blocking further movement." Finally, "the gray whale mother and calf … rolled onto their sides, sank below the surface, and were not sighted alive or dead again," although one orca was noticed to have a large chunk of flesh in its mouth.

There is very little that a single female whale can do to prevent her calf from being attacked by a well-drilled pod of killer whales. One defensive maneuver is to park the calf in a thick bed of kelp in order to hide it. This type of action was once witnessed by BC artist Mark Hobson, who used the scene in one of his favorite paintings. Presumably this type of defense would not work well with transient killer whales, which regularly patrol the kelp beds for otters, seals, and sea lions.

Another form of defense for any species is simply to keep quiet and not broadcast your presence. Philippe Cousteau watched gray whales in Matancitas Lagoon in Baja, and found that "as soon as they had located us, it seemed that all whale sounds in the lagoon ceased instantly." He interpreted this move as "protection against marine animals whose hearing is as keen as their own; against killer whales, for example."

Exhaling underwater in response to killer whales in the area has been reported a number of times. In 1980, two gray whales observed by biologist M.M. Poole dove underwater when five orcas approached, exhaled underwater, and stayed under for seventeen minutes, surfacing only when the orcas left. As orcas use echo-location to hunt, the exhaled bubbles may offer both an acoustic and physical screen that helps hide the whales from the orcas.

One extraordinary defensive move was witnessed by Earl Thomas, a tour boat driver who works out of Tofino, British Columbia. In 1995, Thomas was cruising through Cox Bay, south of Tofino, when he spotted a pod of five killer whales. It was the transient killer whale pod known to biologists as T23 and to locals as The Motley Crew due to the orcas' scars and dorsal fin damage. Also in the bay were a female gray whale and her calf. Suddenly the pod spotted the whale and calf and started toward them. "The next thing I knew," says Thomas, "the mother appeared belly up on the surface of the water beside my boat, with the calf held on her stomach, between her two big flippers." After a few unsuccessful taps on her flippers, the orcas retreated and the mother and calf dove, appearing out of harm's way on the other side of the bay. "It was awesome," says Thomas.

In addition to large predators, gray whales are often bothered by small parasites, and probably carry more parasites than other whale species. Grays are usually covered with the barnacle *Cryptolepas rhachianecti*, which is found only on gray whales. The barnacles are often concentrated on the whales' heads and backs, and are usually found in clusters. The barnacles reach 3.8 centimeters (1.5 inches) in diameter and deeply embed themselves in the whales' outer skin. Barnacle infestations are not a recent addition to the gray whale's list of problems; gray whale barnacles have been found in fossils dating back to the Miocene, over five million years ago.

Whale lice (which are not true lice but tiny crustaceans), including the gray whale louse *Cyamus scammoni* and the more widespread *C. kessleri* and *C. ceti,* usually are found crawling among the barnacles, and feed on dead skin. Strong pincers near the heads of the lice enable them to cling tenaciously to their hosts. The lice are especially common around the blowhole, throat grooves, eyes, ears, genital slit, and anus. They often enter cuts to feed upon the whale's living tissue; one gray whale had 100,000 lice crowded into a large cut on its back. So common are barnacle and lice infestations that the adult gray whale often carries several hundred pounds worth of these pesky parasites.

A closeup of the lice and barnacles carried by a gray whale. (Frank S. Balthis/Nature's Design)

The dead skin that sloughs off the gray's body also attracts small fish, which nibble hungrily at the living buffet. In the Baja calving lagoons, small fish called topsmelt (*Atherinops affinis*) feed on both the skin of whales and whale lice.

One way that gray whales remove parasites and dead skin is through rubbing on gravel on the ocean bottom. Russian observers report that Asian gray whales rub on submerged pebbly beaches, leaving behind shed barnacles. Closer to home, the southeast side of Indian Island near Tofino, British Columbia, has a small bay with a smooth pebbly bottom where grays like to rub. (Other whale species are well-known rubbers. Robson Bight, on the northeast side of Vancouver Island, has been set aside as a preserve for killer whales which rub there.)

Another means of removing barnacles and lice is apparently used by whales in Russia. As early as 1755, Russian biologists have reported gray whales entering brackish water in coastal lagoons and the mouths of rivers in order for the fresh water to kill their marine parasites. There are even unsubstantiated reports of grays swimming under cliffs over which waterfalls tumble into the sea for the same reason.

In addition to problems with external parasites, whales can be afflicted with a wide range of diseases, including cancers, stomach ulcers, heart disease, pneumonia, jaundice, and even arthritis. They are also susceptible to a number of internal worms. Of seventy gray whales once examined by Russian biologist V.V. Zimushko, over half had internal worm infestations.

Every year a few gray whales die due to bizarre natural circumstances, such as those that claimed the life of a yearling female in April 1997. The body of this female was found in a shallow bay on Flores Island, north of Tofino on Vancouver Island. Investigation revealed that the whale's intestine was blocked with sticks, grass, leaves, and branches, along with a scattering of herring roe. It is believed that the unfortunate yearling fed upon the roe that was scattered among the woody debris floating off the mouth of a nearby river, accidentally ingested far too much of the debris, and died of an intestinal blockage.

One unusual situation involving gray whales is the stranding phenomenon, in which whales purposefully or accidentally strand themselves upon beaches. Biologists theorize that there may be numerous reasons for strandings. Many may not be true strandings at all, but merely the result of animals that have died of old age, illness, or accidents washing up on shore through natural wave action. The actions of waves and currents may result in "whale graveyards" such as the Whalers Isles off central Vancouver Island, where local fishermen swear that whales "go to die."

Some strandings may be due to parasitic infestations or diseases which affect the whales' ability to navigate properly. Stranded whales are often found to have flatworms or roundworms in their brains or ear canals; in a 1972 beaching of dolphins in southern California, every single animal was found to be infested with flatworms in the brain.

Occasionally, whales follow food into shallow water and ultimately end up in water too shallow for them to retreat. Many strandings seem to occur at spots where geomagnetic contours cross coastlines at right angles, suggesting that whales were using magnetic intensity to navigate and somehow became confused when land got in the way.

Among strongly social whales like pilot whales, strandings may be due to herd instinct, the result of one lead whale accidentally beaching itself, and its pod members blindly following it. In the Hebrides, Orkney, Shetland, and Faeroe islands, whalers used to take advantage of this blind instinct to catch whales. Dozens of boats would encircle a school of pilot whales and push it toward shallow water. One whale was then harpooned, and when the injured animal ran itself ashore and beached itself, the rest of the school would follow. The whalers could then dispatch the beached whales with harpoons and lances.

It is also possible that harassment by predators is sometimes to blame for strandings, resulting in a whale beaching itself to escape an enemy. In July 1997, a pod of killer whales trapped a group of white-sided dolphins in Codville Lagoon on BC's King

Encounters with boat propellers often result in long slashes on a gray whale's back. (Wilfred Atleo)

This 1874 engraving fancifully shows Arctic waters teeming with summering gray whales. (From The Marine Mammals of the Northwestern Coast of North America by Charles Scammon)

Island. Some of the dolphins stranded themselves upon the beach to escape the jaws of the orcas, and were later saved by local fishermen.

And since whales are known to be attracted to some noises emanating from boat engines, some whales may come into shallow water and then become disoriented by the barrage of noise that surrounds them. A 1979 stranding of sperm whales on the central Oregon coast was blamed by some on the acoustic confusion caused by the engines of a noisy river dredge.

Strandings occur most commonly among toothed whales, and are especially common among pilot whales, false killer whales, and sperm whales. Each year, there are about fourteen strandings by gray whales along the western US coast and two or three along the west coast of Vancouver Island. Between 1950 and 1981, forty-three percent of the ninety-seven known gray whale strandings were by gray whale calves, suggesting that much of the blame for such incidents can be placed on sheer inexperience with strong currents or a lack of strength to fight storms or predators.

Studies in the lagoons of Baja confirm that the highest mortality is among the whale calves. According to studies in San Ignacio Lagoon, 5.4 percent of gray whale calves die within the calving lagoons, and thirty-one percent of the calves that begin the northward migration die before making it as far as southern California. Seventy-five percent of the first-year mortalities occur within the first few weeks of birth. In 1980, almost forty dead gray whale calves were found in Scammon's Lagoon, all of which died from apparently natural causes. From 1980 to 1982, fifty dead gray whale calves were found on the ocean side of Sand Island, a large island which separates Guerrero Negro Lagoon and Scammon's Lagoon from the open ocean. The discovery suggests that many births take place in the open ocean rather than in the lagoons, and that calving mortality might be even higher than lagoon surveys indicate.

Those whales fortunate enough to avoid the numerous perils of life in the wild may live long lives. Grays are aged by counting the annual layers of wax deposited in the ear plugs, each layer consisting of one light and one dark lamina. Of seventy gray whales from the Chukotka Peninsula area examined by Russian biologist V.V. Zimushko, the oldest was a fifty-six-year-old female. Of 316 gray whales taken along the California coast between 1959 and 1969 for scientific research, the oldest was a seventy-year-old male. The maximum lifespan of the gray whale is likely around seventy-five years, a ripe old age for a wandering giant.

Chapter Two Spirit of the Deep

The whale always gives our people something. The whale always helps someone who needs him.
– Native John Thomas (Nitinaht), 1991

When I was a small boy growing up in Calgary, our family had a neighbor who was from a First Nations band. And as a small boy, I often listened in awe to her stories of life on the plains. What especially intrigued me was her attitude toward the wild animals of the plains. Never before had I ever heard an adult talk of a wild animal as our "brother." It was a lesson in respect that I have never forgotten.

All around the Pacific Rim, from Japan north to Siberia and then along the North American coast from Alaska south to Baja California, a number of First Nations and Inuit tribes have both revered and respected the gray whale, the stuff of life and the stuff of legend. It is not known when West Coast aboriginals first began hunting whales, but one archeological site with whale remains at Namu on the central British Columbia coast is at least 9,100 years old.

Aboriginal people used almost every part of the whale, but primarily the oil, blubber, meat, and bone. The oil was used for cooking, as a gravy on foods, and as a fire starter; the meat for food; and the bones for clubs, combs, and roof supports. Whale vertebrae served as chairs. Whale sinews were used to bind harpoons, which ironically were then used to kill more whales. Whale skin was deemed a delicacy by Inuit people.

In Asia, the Koryak people hunted gray whales from skin boats using harpoons and lances. They lived in the northern Okhotsk Sea along the Kamchatka Peninsula. To the east of the peninsula, the Koryaks used nets to catch young grays in shallow

FACING PAGE: *An Indian hunter with skin floats at his feet, fastening on a harpoon point.*
(BC Archives: #D-09032)

The soaring dorsal fin on this statue by Bill Reid, which sits outside the Vancouver Public Aquarium, identifies it as a killer whale.
(Robert H. Busch)

bays. Before a hunt, they wore special masks to dances in which they invoked whale spirits. In these dances, the Koryaks confessed any sins they had committed, asking for forgiveness, clearly elevating the whales to the level of an all-knowing and all-forgiving god.

The Comte de Lacépède described in his 1804 book *Histoire Naturelle des Cetaces* the hunting habits of unnamed native Siberians in the Kamchatka Peninsula area: "Throughout the fall, the inhabitants of several islands near Kamchatka set out in search of whales, which are plentiful just offshore at that time of year. When they come across any ... they ... stab them with poisoned spears." According to some accounts, the Kerek and Kurile people, who lived northeast of the Koryaks, both used poisoned weapons to hunt grays.

The use of poison on whale harpoons is also ascribed to several other tribes around the Pacific Rim, who may have dipped their harpoons in poisonous aconite, made from the monkshood plant. The root was powdered, mixed with water, and allowed to ferment to a poisonous concentrate. These tribes set out in two-man canoes in the frigid Bering and Chukchi seas to hunt whales. Once harpooned, a whale took many days to die, for aconite is a weak poison. They did not tow the dead whale to shore like most West Coast aboriginals, but waited for the huge corpse to float ashore. While they were waiting, rituals were performed asking the spirits to bring the whale in from the sea.

The greatest numbers of grays were taken along the coast of the Chukotka Peninsula, the extreme northeast tip of Asia. There the Chukchi and Mechigmen people built settlements and memorials from the bones of gray whales. In the Masik settlement, at the entry to Mechigmen Inlet, archeologists have found over a thousand skulls of young gray whales. Most belonged to young calves only six to eight months old. The Chukotka settlement at Lorino has been a major aboriginal gray whaling center right up to modern times.

The Aleut of Alaska, who called the gray whale *chickakhluk*, guarded the secret of the aconite jealously and made up wild tales to mislead early anthropologists and missionaries. One story was that they used the putrid fat from a human corpse as a poison, a fairy tale that was believed and reported as fact by nineteenth-century anthropologists Pinart and Veniaminov.

Harpoon tips of slate were used by the Aleuts, who believed that slate itself was poisonous. The Aleuts both hunted whales and used stranded ones. Veniaminov reported that most Aleut villages were on the north side of the Aleut Islands because whales drifted ashore there. However, the Aleuts would not touch a whale that had decayed, and could detect this state by the absence of a certain species of bird on the carcass.

Northern Alaskan Inuit, who called the gray whale *antokhak*, would bring out whale figurines made of wood, bone, or ivory before a whale hunt. They sang songs to the figurines asking for luck in the hunt. Then they would dance, mimicking the great whales, and would take water tinted a deep red into their mouths, spouting it into the air like a harpooned whale spouting blood. Of the Inuit, Captain Charles Scammon wrote in 1874, "The choicest pieces [of the whale] for a dainty repast, for them, are the flukes, lips, and fins."

Off the south coast of Alaska, the Koniag people of Kodiak Island occasionally hunted whales, as did their neighbors to the east, the Chugash. Along the southeast coast of Alaska, the Tlingit apparently never hunted whales, but occasionally used stranded ones, as did the Haida of the Queen Charlotte Islands and the Tsimshian on the BC coast.

Further south, First Nations people of Vancouver Island and Washington's Olympic Peninsula were avid whalers. They believed that "Whale People" lived in human form in undersea houses, and that when they emerged from their houses, they took the form of whales. Whales that washed up dead were scrounged for meat, oil, and bones. But the Natives also often took to the sea to hunt the great whales.

Among the Nootka people of Vancouver Island, the highest-ranking males prepared for a whale hunt by going into the forest and swimming in sacred ponds, spouting like a whale. According to John R. Jewitt, a sailor captured by Nootka warriors,

Native representation of the gray whale

West Coast Natives used long cedar canoes to hunt gray whales. (Parks Canada)

the head of the tribe went into the woods three times to sing and pray. Anthropologist E.S. Curtis recorded one of the Nootkan prayers: "Whale, I want you to come near me so that I will get hold of your heart and deceive it." After the third time in the woods, the chief fasted for two days. Arriving back in the village, the high-ranking males said prayers and chants asking the gods for luck in the whale hunt. In the week before the hunt, the hunters all bathed several times a day and abstained from sex, a curious practice still followed by some athletes today.

The whale hunters often went to sea just before sunset, and rested at sea until dawn when the hunt commenced. While pursuing a whale by eight-man canoe, the chief of the tribe would sing songs to the whale, asking it to come closer and referring to it reverently as "ruler of the world." The whale was harpooned with a yew-wood harpoon with a mussel-shell tip. If the whale swam away from shore, the hunters would sing and chant, imploring the spirits to be more kind. Occasionally a wooden knife was used to cut the tendons to the whale's tail flukes, crippling the animal. Once the whale tired, it was killed with a short lance and towed to shore. Four sealskin floats attached to the harpoon line helped to keep the carcass afloat.

On the beach, the whale was sometimes covered with duck and eagle feathers, and prayers of thanks were given to the gods. Then the whale was carved up, with pieces going to the hunters in sizes proportional to their rank in the tribe. The whale oil was rendered by boiling chunks of blubber in long wooden tubs heated by hot stones placed inside. Following a feast of whale meat, the

Nootkas did dances of thanksgiving for their good fortune.

Captain Charles Scammon wrote about the aboriginals of Vancouver Island in his 1874 book *The Marine Mammals of the Northwestern Coast of North America*, stating: "Those among them who could boast of killing a whale formerly had the most exalted mark of honor conferred upon them by a cut across the nose."

Like many hunters, aboriginal whalers often met with frustration. Maquinna, a Vancouver Island chief in the 1700s, once spent fifty-three days at sea, harpooning eight whales, but only landing one. Other sources estimate that for every one they killed Natives lost five to ten whales, often due to harpoons that broke upon impacting a whale's mighty back.

As much as the whale was a vital source of food to aboriginal peoples, it was also an item of respect. The people of Ahousat, north of Tofino on the west coast of Vancouver Island, were said to sacrifice a slave in honor of the first whale killed in each season. The Tse-shaht people on Vancouver Island called the whale *Ee-toop*, and sang a song to it during the great potlatches, the days of feasting and gift exchanges later outlawed by white missionaries. "I search for Ee-toop," they sang, "bigness, largeness, the mass that moves upon the seas."

It would appear that both gray and humpback whales were pursued by aboriginal hunters. In the Clayoquot Sound area on Vancouver Island, barnacles specific to humpback whales are more commonly found in Indian middens. But further south, at La Push, Washington, the predominant bones in Indian middens are those of gray whales.

Whales are a common feature on many BC aboriginal artifacts. The humpback whale can be recognized by its huge flippers. The killer whale is denoted by a soaring dorsal fin. The gray whale can be recognized on artifacts by its long narrow shape, small flippers, and lack of a dorsal fin. Inevitably, the gray whale was occa-

Whales were often depicted on Native totem poles.
(Robert H. Busch)

sionally featured on totem poles erected by various tribes along the northwest coast. On the poles, the gray was depicted by a short dorsal fin and a long slender form dappled with painted spots to represent barnacles.

Even in recent times, the gray has been part of ceremonial totems. In the We-Wai-Kum Band cemetery at Campbell River on Vancouver Island, a totem was erected in 1978 by local carver Sam Henderson. In the middle of the pole is a carved whale, with tail flukes curved over its back, a tiny dorsal fin, and large round dapples on its back. Chances are, the whale is supposed to be a gray.

Whales have also been featured on petroglyphs carved into rocks along the west coast. One little-known site is at Quisitis Point, just south of the Wickaninnish Interpretive Centre in Pacific Rim National Park. A rubbing of the petroglyph can be seen high on the wall within the Centre. Another is at Cape Alava in Washington.

One of the best-documented aboriginal bands along the west coast is the Makah of the Olympic Peninsula of northern Washington, who anxiously awaited the arrival of migrating gray whales each year. The Makah called the gray whales *sih-wah-wihw*, meaning "beings with itchy faces." To attract whales, the chiefs and their wives would fast and bathe in secret prayer ponds just as their Nootka cousins up north did. In these ponds, they would swim slowly, in hopes that the whales would do the same. They also mimicked spouting whales, taking water into their mouths, and spraying it out while praying to the whales.

The Makah made whaling harpoons out of elk antlers or yew wood, with a sharpened mussel shell as the tip. Sentries posted on high vantage points were used to spot whales. Upon hearing of a whale sighting, the men of the tribe set out in eleven-meter (36-foot) cedar canoes. The wives of the hunters stayed home, lying on their backs in their longhouses, absolutely still, in hopes that the whales would also be docile. Realizing that the great beasts were difficult to kill, the Makah tried to lance them in the shoulder behind the flip-

Detail of the whale on this totem pole, carved by Charlie Mickey of the Hesquiat Band in 1972.
(Robert H. Busch)

per, where a vital lung or heart might be hit. Only the chief or his son was allowed to harpoon a whale. (Most historians believe that the first Makah men bold enough to chase whales became chiefs and created a hereditary rulership.) Occasionally, an ambitious hunter would leap onto a whale's back to harpoon it. Attached to the harpoons were thirty-meter (100-foot) lines with inflated sealskin floats at their ends. The floats served to slow down the whales as they slowly bled to death.

As soon as the whale slowed down, hunters would dive into the frigid water and sew its mouth closed with cedar-bark rope. This sealed in buoyant gases and helped

An artist's rendition of a Nootka whale hunt in the stormy Pacific. (Parks Canada)

The whale is often used in modern Native art, such as this painting by Washington artist Joe David in the Tin Wis Resort Lodge, Tofino, BC. (Robert H. Busch)

to prevent their catch from sinking. The whale was then towed to shore for butchering. The Makah mainly used the oil and bones, generally avoiding the meat as it spoils rapidly. On shore, the dead whale was greeted with songs and treated as an honored guest in hopes it would come again to the tribe. According to some accounts, the Makah and other Northwest aboriginals frequently used whale oil as a trading commodity. According to H.H. Bancroft, the Makah sold $8,000 worth of whale oil in 1856.

The whale figured prominently in the myths and stories of the Makah people and was the salvation of many a tribe over the long hungry winters. According to one story:

> *Thunderbird flew down and just as he was about to hit the water, he swooped back up carrying a whale in his talons. He flew toward the village. He flew close to the beach and there he dropped the whale. Then he flew away. The man who saw all this said to the people, 'We're saved, we're saved.'*

Such was the respect that bound the Makah to the whale.

The next bands south of the Makah were the Quileute and Quinault, who occasionally hunted grays. Further south again were the Klallam, who heavily depended upon salmon. According to one early anthropologist, the Klallam "[did] not go out to sea hunting for whales as [did] the Makah and Nootka, but wait[ed] until one [was] in sight."

South of Washington, the next group of aboriginals that used whales was the Chumash, who lived in the Channel Islands and coastal southern California. Although there is one account of the Chumash hunting whales, most anthropologists believe they only used stranded whales.

Pre-Columbian aboriginals as far south as Baja California hunted whales with some regularity, as shown by a cave painting in the hills above Bahia Magdalena of a whale with a number of harpoons sticking out of it. Bahia Magdalena, on the west coast of Baja, is one of the three top nursing and breeding areas for gray whales in North America, so it is quite likely that the whale in the painting is a gray whale.

The last First Nations gray whale hunt using the old ceremonial ways took place off the coast of Washington in 1928. Today, very few of the West Coast aboriginals are interested in hunting whales. As one Nuu-Chah-Nulth Native told me, "Those days belong to our ancestors now, and even they are now spirits."

Chapter Three   Of Whales and Men

Concerning the whale's valor, we do find that he is not very courageous ... for if he sees a man
or a longboat he goeth underwater and runs away.
— Frederick Martens, German whaler, 1671

Man is one of the greediest animals on Earth. Our attitude toward many of our fellow creatures is not one of peaceful coexistence, but wholesale exploitation. In the case of the gray whale, mankind's greed and lack of foresight has resulted in the complete extinction of the Atlantic population of gray whales and the near-extinction of the population on the west side of the Pacific Ocean. The only gray whale population that is thriving is that on the east side of the Pacific, and even it has been driven almost to extinction on two occasions. All in all, it is not a record of which mankind can be proud.

But in recent years, a new brand of human has emerged as our appreciation of the wild world matures. Whale-watching is now a big business, and thousands of people annually thrill to see the incredible breach of a whale. Others trek to aquariums for a closeup view of smaller whales and dolphins, and from that experience comes a new respect for cetaceans.

In only two decades we have gone from whale hunters to whale lovers, and the seas are a better place for all creatures because of it. I like to think that the bad old days of animal exploitation are gone, are a bit of ugly history that we have buried in our past. But in the past six years of making a living as a nature writer, I have found that mankind still has a long way to go to reach a state of harmony with our wild neighbors. In the very recent past I have read of a cruise ship found guilty of dumping garbage into the pristine waters off Alaska, of a wildlife trader charged with illegally

FACING PAGE: *An eighteenth-century engraving of a Basque trying village.* (Archives F.R.L.)

trying to import orangutans into Singapore, and of a local logging company that was given a stiff fine for violations of the provincial forestry code. All of these things bother me. But when I really think of it, would these situations have been news items in the sixties? Would we even have had laws against these practices in the seventies? Did some of the conservation magazines in which I read these reports even exist in the eighties? I can only hope that one day we will look back at the nineties and say with pride that that was when humans and animals finally learned to share the Earth.

The Korean Gray Whale

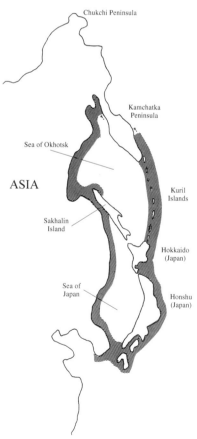

Historic range of the Korean gray whale.

Chukchi Peninsula

Kamchatka Peninsula

Sea of Okhotsk

ASIA

Kuril Islands

Sakhalin Island

Hokkaido (Japan)

Sea of Japan

Honshu (Japan)

Off the northeast coast of Asia lives a stock of gray whales which is barely clinging to survival. It is likely that this stock never numbered more than about five thousand individuals, but today it is down to a couple of hundred, barely enough to keep the stock alive. Some biologists believe that the so-called Korean stock was originally divided into two groups. One group traveled south along the coast of Asia, hugging the Sea of Okhotsk and Sea of Japan down to the southern shore of South Korea. The other may have traveled south from the Kamchatka Peninsula along the Kuril Islands and east coast of Japan to Kyushu, the southernmost island of Japan.

Whaling in Japan began many centuries ago, if a tenth-century poem describing the catching of whales by small boat is to be believed. The Korean stock of gray whales was first exploited in the 1600s, when Japanese whalers started to roam over the inshore Asian waters. Originally the Japanese pursued the gray whale with hand-held harpoons, but in 1675 a new method of whaling with nets was developed. Gray whalers later changed to lances when they discovered the female whales' ferocity in defending their young. They dubbed the gray whale *koku kujira*, meaning devilfish, as a result. A 1758 Treatise of the Whale contains the earliest known Japanese drawing of the gray whale, accurately depicting its barnacle scars, linear shape, and short bristles on the snout and jaw.

Part of the Japanese taste for whale meat derives from religious beliefs: both Shintoism and Buddhism frown on the eating of meat from mammals, but whales

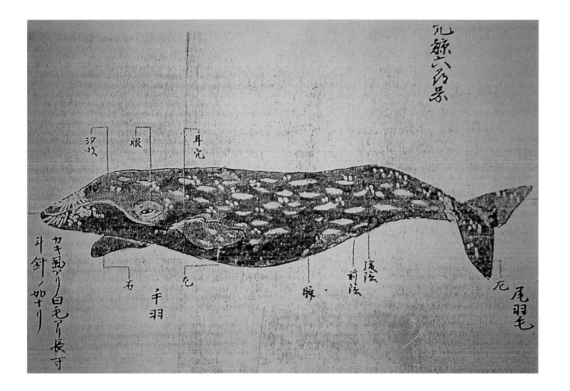

An early Japanese drawing of the gray whale, dated 1661–1673, from A History of Whaling at Taijiura, Kumano.
(Japan Whaling Association)

were considered fish. Even after 1758, when a Japanese naturalist correctly classed whales as mammals, they were considered fish for dietary reasons. Although the meat of the whale was considered the most valuable part of the whale, almost every part was used. An 1829 cookbook entitled *Kujira Chomi Ho* (How to Prepare Whale) stated that the choicest parts were the eyes and mammary glands.

In the early days of Japanese whaling, the boats were few and far between, and the Korean gray whale was able to withstand the hunting pressures. It is estimated that from the seventeenth to the nineteenth centuries, an average of only about twenty grays a year were taken. The peak harvest years from the limited records appear to be 1869 to 1878.

THOMPSON-NICOLA REGIONAL DISTRICT LIBRARY SYSTEM

Gray whale killed by whalers in Korea, 1912. (Roy C. Andrews/ Dept. of Library Services, American Museum of Natural History, neg. #218422)

The advent of modern whaling ships in Japan in 1898 spelled doom to the stock as the demand for whale meat soon pushed the Korean gray whale to the brink of extinction. (Whale meat is still a delicacy in Japan, and sells for about $45 a pound. Tail meat is known as *ono-mi* and is used raw in sushi.) It is thought that the gray whale was gone from the shores of Japan by 1914. Korean whaling ships took about fifteen hundred gray whales between 1910 and 1933, by which point the grays off Korea were almost extirpated as well.

Fortunately, the Pacific Ocean is a big place, and a few sightings of gray whales in Asian waters between 1942 and 1979 proved that the stock was still hanging on: single whales were sighted in 1942 north of the Kuril Islands; in 1959 near Sakhalin

Island and near Shingu on the southern coast of Japan; in 1967 in the Okhotsk Sea; in 1968 southeast of Honshu, with an accidental capture of a young female gray near Shingu; in 1974 in the Okhotsk Sea; in 1978 near Vladimir's Bay; and in 1979 near the southeastern tip of the Kamchatka Peninsula. That same year, two grays were seen near Furugelm Island.

By 1980, biologists began to wonder if the Asian gray whale was heading for extinction, for the trickle of sightings disappeared. One 1982 book went so far as to state that the Asian gray was "virtually extinct." Then, in October 1983, Russian biologists with the Research Institute of Fishing and Oceanography discovered twenty gray whales near Pil'tun Zaliv, a coastal town on the northeast coast of Sakhalin Island. This was the largest sighting of Asian gray whales in over fifty years.

A few years later, a large group of grays was discovered near the Kuril Islands northeast of Japan and the population estimate was revised once more. In 1994 and 1995, Russian scientists photographed about thirty-eight individual whales on their feeding grounds northeast of Sakhalin Island. Today, the Asian gray whale is thought to range from Korea north to the Kamchatka Peninsula. It undergoes a similar migration to that of its North American cousins, summering in the Sea of Okhotsk and trekking south to breeding grounds around the Korean peninsula in the winter.

No one knows if the Korean gray whale interbreeds with North American grays, which are right next door each summer, although current DNA work by San Diego–based biologists may soon resolve that question. (According to Alexey Yablokov, a biologist with the Academy of Sciences of the USSR, "one can assume that at the present time the populations of the California and Korean gray whales do not overlap," but no one knows for sure.) The details of its life are still a mystery for one simple reason: there are too few Korean gray whales left to study, a tragic situation for such a noble animal. However, the tide may be turning for the Korean gray whale as conservationists try to save the race and as Asians in general slowly become more conservation minded. Whale-watching in Japan is now a $9-million-a-year business, and one can only hope that the gray whale will benefit from the new attitude toward it.

The Atlantic Gray Whale

Few people are aware that gray whales once lived in the Atlantic Ocean as well as the Pacific. In fact, some biologists believe that the gray whale first evolved in the North Atlantic Ocean, spreading to the North Pacific during a period of warm temperatures, when migration through the Arctic was easier. Dubbed *Eschrichtius gibbosus gibbosus* by early biologists, the Atlantic gray whale once roamed both sides of the Atlantic. In European waters the Atlantic gray whale was pushed to extinction by the fourteenth century. In North American waters it hung on a bit longer, and is thought to have lasted until about 1750. The Atlantic gray whale is thought to have ranged in North America from the Gulf of Mexico north to the waters off Greenland and Iceland, but the exact limits of its former distribution, as well as its original numbers, are unknown.

The whaling industry off the east coast of North America began with the arrival of Basque whalers in the late 1400s, although some authorities believe that they may have reached North American shores as early as 1372. (A tombstone recently found in Newfoundland bearing a Basque inscription that dates from the late 1300s would certainly support that belief.) The Basques hailed from the Bay of Biscay area off the coast of France and Spain (Bay of Biscay means Bay of Basques).

The Basques began commercial whaling off the coast of Europe as early as the ninth century and were the predominant European whalers by the eleventh century. In fact, the word harpoon comes from the Basque word *arpoi* (meaning "stone point"), which became *arpon* in Spanish and then harpoon in English. By 1450, the Basques were whaling from the Azores north to Iceland, and it was only a matter of time before they wandered even farther and reached North America. One story says that Columbus first learned of the New World from a Basque whaler.

The municipal archives of the town of Biarritz contain letters written in 1511 authorizing French Basques to search for whales in the New World. When Jacques Cartier sailed into the Gulf of St. Lawrence in 1534, the Basque town of Buterus in Labrador was already extant, listed on French maps as *Hable de la Ballaine* (Harbour of the Whales). The northern tip of Newfoundland was described on maps as *Karpont*, a

FACING PAGE:
Early mapmakers often drew fanciful representations of whales such as this one on a map by Jacques le Moyne de Morgues, drawn after his 1864 trip to Florida.
(Archives E.R.L.)

corruption of its original Basque name Cap Arpont (Cape Harpoon). One anonymous mid-1500s record stated that the worst risk to navigation in the New Founde Land was the abundance of whales in the area.

By the mid 1500s, the Basques were a well-established presence in eastern Canada, with forty to fifty whaling stations along the Strait of Belle Isle between Labrador and Newfoundland. The stations stretched from Middle Bay, Quebec, up the coast to Cape Charles, Labrador. One of the largest of the shore stations was at Red Bay, Labrador. In 1977, archeologists began exploring the site and found a rich trove of Basque artifacts. They determined that at Red Bay's peak, in the 1560s and 1570s, nearly a thousand men worked the nearby waters to produce a half-million gallons of whale oil.

The Basques pursued whales in small boats called *chalupas*, which were eight meters (26 feet) long and held six rowers. The whales were spotted by lookout stations called *atalayas* located on the tops of hills overlooking the ocean. Piles of burning wet straw alerted the whaling boats to the presence of the whales. When a whale was harpooned, a floating wooden drag called a *drogue* was attached to the end of the line to tire the beast out. A quick lance to the heart or lungs ended its misery. The carcass was then towed to shore and cut up. Chunks of blubber were cooked in furnaces called try-works. One such furnace excavated in the 1980s was nine meters (30 feet) long, big enough to hold six huge copper cauldrons in which the whale oil was boiled off. An anonymous eighteenth-century account described the cooking process:

This engraving from Henry H. Brownwell's The English in America *(1861) shows the incredible black smoke emanating from on-board try-works on a Pacific whaling ship.*

First they stoke the fire with wood; then they switch to unrendered blubber, which burns very hot. After the whale has been ... stripped of all its blubber, the baleen ... are sliced out of its maw. The ... crew of each ship receives half the proceeds from the oil; the captain, pilot, and flensers receive ... the proceeds from the baleen as a bonus.

The oil was stored in wooden barrels and shipped on large galleons back to Europe. The average galleon carried a cargo of about 227,000 liters (50,000 gallons) of oil, worth about $4 million in today's dollars.

Although most of the whales taken by the Basques seem to have been right whales and bowheads, it is thought that gray whales must have been taken as well, for some of the long, thin whales described by early Basque whalers could only have been grays. In addition, sixteenth- and seventeenth-century accounts of gray whales by Basques could only have referred to North American grays, for the species was extinct by that time in European waters.

The Basques called the gray whale the *sandloegja* or *otta sotta*. A 1611 Basque description of the *otta sotta* stated that it had "the same color as the Trumpa {sperm whale}" and had "finnes {baleen} in its mouth ... not above halfe a yard long." The *otta sotta* did not produce the best whale oil nor the greatest quantity of oil (about a third as much as from a right whale). The Basques listed whales in order of commercial appeal; the *otta sotta* only managed to place fourth on the list. A 1640 description of the *sandloegja* was an interesting mix of fact and fancy: "It has white baleen plates ... It is very tenacious of life and can come on land to lie as seal{s} like to rest the whole day."

In less than fifty years, Basque whalers in the New World killed at least 15,000 whales of all types. Word of success spreads fast among fishermen, and news of the rich New World whaling grounds soon reached the rest of Europe. In 1598, Queen Elizabeth I sent a whaling fleet to Greenland. By 1611, the Muscovy Company of London was pursuing whales off that same massive island. Soon these whalers began to trek south to waters off the coast of New England.

Whales were once common in New England waters. The *Mayflower* pilgrims noted in 1620 that "large whales ... came daily alongside and played about the ship." Richard Mather wrote in 1635 of "multitudes of great whales ... spewing up water in the air... making the sea about them white and hoary." In 1705, a missionary noted that whales off the coast of New Brunswick and Nova Scotia were "in such abundance [and] came so close to the land they could be harpooned from the rocks."

According to some sources, the Natives of the east coast had long hunted the Atlantic gray whale, which they called the *powdaree*. Captain George Weymouth, who explored the Maine coast in 1605, described one such whale hunt:

> They go in company of their king in a multitude of their boats; and
> strike him with a bone made in a fashion of a harping iron, fastened
> to a rope; which they make great and strong of bark of trees; ... with
> their arrows they shoot him to death.

Wounded whales were sometimes tied to floating logs to slow them down until they died of their injuries. Some historians doubt the accuracy of accounts such as Captain Weymouth's. Elizabeth Little, with the Nantucket Historical Association, says, "I can find no evidence that Indians of New England routinely killed whales at sea." She has, however, confirmed that Indians harvested dead whales washed onto the shore, a practice called drift whaling.

Drift whaling grew to be of great local importance to many early settlements along the east coast. By 1644, the townsfolk of Southampton had written rules for sharing "such whales as were by hard luck and the kindness of Providence cast up." Many of the places that were the best sites for drift whaling soon turned into the spots where near-shore whalers set up shop. According to Elizabeth Little, near-shore or along-shore whaling began in Delaware as early as 1632 and soon worked its way along the coast.

Commercial whaling off the east coast of the United States is thought to have begun in 1632 in Long Island Sound, when Dutch whalers established themselves there. At one time, Long Island Sound supported high numbers of whales. A memo-

Whaling off Long Island. An engraving by W.P. Bodfish, from Harper's Weekly, 31 January 1885. (Peabody Essex Museum, Salem, MA, USA)

randum in the British Secretary of State's papers for 1667 states that "The sea was rich in whales near Delaware Bay, but … they were to be found in greater numbers about the end of Long Island." In 1669, the whaler Samuel Mavericke took thirteen gray whales off Long Island and noted that there were so many around that several could be seen in the harbor every day. By 1687, there were seven small whaling factories along the Southampton and Easthampton beaches of Long Island. In 1707, those factories produced over 6,000 barrels of gray whale oil. As the average gray whale produced about thirty-six barrels of oil, this single year accounted for a catch of almost 200 gray whales.

When the Dutch handed Long Island over to the English, it became part of the territory of the Duke of York. Under the "Duke's Laws," whales were declared a "royal fish." A fifteenth of a gallon of whale oil was reserved as a tax payable to the Duke for any whales "cast upon the Shoare of any Precinct."

In 1658, British settlers led by Thomas Macy purchased Nantucket Island near Cape Cod for thirty pounds sterling and two beaver hats. Fourteen years later, the residents of Nantucket killed a large whale trapped in their harbor. According to Obediah Macy, a descendant of Thomas, this first whale killed in Nantucket was a gray whale. From this humble beginning grew the start of a thriving whaling industry. Whaling in Nantucket boomed in 1680 and reached its peak in 1726, by which time the nearest waters were severely depleted of whales. According to Zaccheus Macy, writing in 1792, "the business lasted pretty good until about 1760, and then the whales gon and pretty much don."

These early inshore whalers took their lives in their hands every time they set out to sea in their small wooden boats. Just picture the task of maneuvering a six-meter (20-foot) boat near enough to a twelve-meter (40-foot) whale in pitching stormy seas in order to harpoon it. The whalers' colorful lives were paralleled with an equally colorful language. The act of lancing the heart or lung of a whale was known as "tapping the claret bottle," named for the scarlet plume of blood which resulted from a kill. When a whale's blowhole spouted blood, the whale was said to be "running up a red flag."

Of course, sometimes the great whales fought back, with devastating results.

The dangerous life of early American whalers is clearly depicted in this artwork by J.S. Ryder, aptly entitled "A Perilous Ride." (The Kendall Whaling Museum, Sharon, MA, USA)

According to one account:

> *Sometimes in the immediate impulse of rage, she will attack the boat and demolish it with one stroke of her tail. In an instant the frail vehicle disappears and the assailants are immersed in the dreadful element.*

Whale products reached their zenith in the sixteenth and seventeenth centuries. Whale oil fueled the lamps of Europe and New England and was used as a lubricant, cooking oil, and in soaps. The springy baleen, known incorrectly as "whalebone," was used in corset stays, umbrella ribs, walking canes, plumes for military helmets, bristles for shaving brushes, and springs for toys. The meat was fed to livestock and to pets, and whalebone was ground up for bone meal. In the early days of whaling, the whale was a swimming storehouse of riches.

New Englanders called the Atlantic gray whale the scrag whale, a name which originated with naturalist Paul Dudley, who first used it in 1725. Dudley was also one of the first to describe the Atlantic gray whale, accurately calling it "near a-kin to the Fin-back, but, instead of a Fin upon his Back, the ridge of the Afterpart of his back is scragged with a Dozen Knobs or Knuckles." The name survives today in a number of Scrag Rocks, -Isles, -Bays, and -Ledges. The millionaire's enclave of Sag Harbor on Long Island was originally Scrag Harbor.

The booming whaling industry in New England spelled the end of the Atlantic gray whale and the increasing lack of inshore whales soon forced whalers to take to deeper waters to search for the mighty sperm whale. The *Boston Newsletter* of March 20, 1727 reported that "We hear from the Towne of Cape [Cod] that the Whale-fishery amongst them [has] failed much this Winter, as it has done for several winters past."

By 1750, the Atlantic gray whale was probably extinct. In 1782, J.H. St. John listed the whales known at Nantucket: right whales, sperm whales, humpback whales, finback whales, and blue whales. But not gray whales. The animal remained only a memory until a fossil Atlantic gray whale was found at Graso, on the coast of Sweden, in 1861. The remains were described by W. Lilljeborg, and his write-up became the first scientific mention of the gray whale.

The California Gray Whale

As whales became scarce in inshore Atlantic waters, it was inevitable that whalers would strike out far to sea. Eventually these ships ventured to untouched southern waters. In 1789, the ship *Emilia* became the first whaler to round the southern tip of South America. Both the master and first mate of the ship were experienced Nantucket whalers. Samuel Enderby, the *Emilia's* owner, wrote that "many owners had declared they shall wait till they hear whether our ship is likely to succeed there." And succeed it did: on March 3, 1789, it killed its first South Pacific whale.

Other whalers soon joined the hunt and quickly spread up the west coast of South America and out into the open ocean as far as Hawaii. By 1793, an English whaling ship had surveyed for whales as far north as Cabo San Lucas at the southern tip of Baja California.

By 1809, New England whalers were hunting sperm whales off the coast of Baja. Some looked farther north. By 1834, there were so many whalers off Vancouver Island that the Hudson's Bay Company considered opening another trading post just to provision them. Many of the whales taken by these early whalers were gray whales, as they cruised close to shore and were easily spotted. Ironically, at about the same time that whaling on the west coast of North America was taking off, the development of cottonseed and rapeseed oils pushed down the price of whale oil.

In 1848, the discovery of Arctic bowhead whales by Captain Thomas Welcome Roys caused many whalers to move north, and the pressure on the gray whale eased somewhat.

Off the lower coast of California, Captain J.P. Davenport began taking gray whales in 1854. Nine years earlier, a pair of ships had entered Magdalena Bay (then called Marguerita Bay) on the west coast of Baja and killed thirty-two gray whales, but the hunt for Baja's grays did not really boom until 1858. That year can be marked as the start of the gray whale's rapid decline in North America, and it was all due to the actions of one man.

Captain Charles Scammon, the whaling captain responsible for the popularity of the Baja whaling lagoons. (From The Marine Mammals of the Northwestern Coast of North America by Charles Scammon)

Captain Charles Melville Scammon was born in Maine and left the New England shores in 1849 for the new whaling waters off California. In 1856, he made his first gray-whaling trip to Magdalena Bay and tasted the excitement of the gray whale hunt for the first time. Stories from ranchers, traders, and aboriginals told of a larger lagoon to the north of Magdalena Bay where even greater numbers of gray whales could be found, and Scammon decided to follow up the stories. In the fall of 1857, he left San Francisco on the brig *Boston* and headed south to Baja California.

When he discovered the entrance to Laguna Ojo de Liebre (Jack Rabbit Spring Lagoon), he at first could not enter as the winds died, stranding him and his crew. But the next morning, they succeeded in pushing the *Boston* through the narrow entrance passage. As soon as he entered the lagoon, Scammon encountered hundreds of gray whales, and thought he had struck it rich.

In that first winter of catching whales in the lagoon, Scammon rendered down seven hundred barrels of oil from about twenty gray whales. His methods of capture were at first very crude. Upon spotting a whale, a whale-boat was lowered off the side of the mother ship and rowed close to the great beast. A harpoon was thrown from the bow of the whale-boat, and the dead whale was then towed ashore for butchering. Calves were often harpooned to lure in their mothers.

Scammon soon found, however, that the female grays were fierce mothers, ramming the small boats, and injuring half of his crew. As he reported later,

> *Our situation was both singular and trying ... the objects of pursuit,*
> *which had been so anxiously sought, were now in countless numbers*
> *about us. It was readily seen that it was impossible to capture the*
> *whales in the usual manner.*

And so Scammon changed his tactics. Instead of using the boats' shoulder-held explosive bomb-lances to finish off the whales, he decided to use them instead of harpoons to secure the whale first. His plan worked incredibly well. Scammon reported that when he returned to San Francisco, his ship was "so deeply laden that her scuppers [drains at the edge of the deck] were washed by the rippling tide." He took so much oil that he filled every vessel aboard ship, including bread casks, with the precious fluid.

Word soon spread of the rich lagoon whaling grounds, and on his second trip to the lagoon, Scammon was accompanied by six other boats. These large brigs anchored just outside the lagoon entrances, and sent their smaller whale-boats into the shallow lagoons to hunt gray whales. The lagoons soon became crowded as twenty-five to thirty whale-boats criss-crossed the water pursuing their targets. Bomb-lance lines became tangled up, boats were overturned, and dead whales floated everywhere. Flags were planted in their backs to identify to which boat they belonged. Abandoned carcasses were known as "stinkers" for obvious reasons, and these were eagerly snared by Mexican natives who lined the shores. In the heydays of the Baja whaling lagoons, whalers from as far away as Hawaii, England, France, and Russia joined in the hunt.

Scammon described the scene of slaughter as "exceedingly picturesque and unusually exciting," an attitude which he held for many years. He described the whales as "exceedingly wild and difficult to approach," and many men were killed by mother whales attempting to defend their young. Scammon reported that in one year alone, "two boats were entirely destroyed, while the others were staved fifteen times."

After only two seasons of lagoon whaling, the catch began to decline, and whalers spread south to the lagoons at San Ignacio and Magdalena Bay. Ironically enough, the former had been discovered by Jared F. Poole, who was Charles Scammon's brother-in-law. Scammon reported that "every navigable lagoon of the region was discovered and explored, and the animals were hunted in every winding and intricate estuary." In his diary, he noted that "in the seasons of 1858 and 1859, not only the bays and lagoons were teeming [with whalers], but the outside coast was lined with ships from San Diego southward to Cape St. Lucas [Cabo San Lucas]."

It is estimated that in Magdalena Bay, between 1845 and 1848, five hundred gray whales were killed. As the Bay became better known, whaling intensified, and between 1854 and 1865, at least fifteen hundred grays were killed. Scammon's Lagoon suffered the same fate: between 1858 and 1860, over one thousand gray whales

"Thar she blows!" Before the advent
of airplanes and helicopters, lookouts
perched on the tops of whaling ships
were used to spot whales.
(BC Archives: #C-06065)

died. Outside the lagoons, whaling ships hunted the gray whales as they entered or left the lagoons, taking almost a thousand whales between 1845 and 1865. The actual kill was even higher, for calves were rarely counted in the catch statistics. As most of the whales taken were females of breeding age, the slaughter had dire consequences for the entire gray whale population.

Scammon's last season as a whaler was in 1863. After a short stint with the US Revenue Cutter Service, the precursor to the Coast Guard, he retired to a farm in California and wrote a fascinating memoir, *The Marine Mammals of the Northwestern Coast of North America, Together With an Account of the American Whale-Fishery*, which was published in San Francisco by John H. Carmany and Company in 1874. In the book, Scammon reported that "the large bays and lagoons, where these animals once congregated, brought forth, and nurtured their young, are already nearly deserted."

Even though the book is a valuable historical record of early whaling, it was a financial failure. The last unsold copies were lost in the great San Francisco fire of 1906. (Today, a first edition of the book is a collector's item, worth thousands of dollars.) Scammon died in California in 1911. The Laguna Ojo de Liebre was renamed Scammon's Lagoon in his honor.

At the same time that whalers were pursuing gray whales in Baja lagoons, shore-based whalers chased the migrating grays off the coast of California. Shore-based whaling began in Monterey in 1854 and soon spread up and down the California coast. These stations specialized in catching whales within 15 kilometers (10 miles) of shore using 8-meter (28-foot) boats and six-man crews. Most boats went out in pairs for safety reasons. The whales killed offshore were towed to the shore stations for butchering.

Captain Charles Scammon described one of these stations vividly:

> Under a precipitous bluff ... is the station. Nearby are the try-works,
> sending forth volumes of thick, black smoke. A little to one side is the ...
> store house ... Boats are hanging from davits, some resting on the quay,
> while others ... swing at their moorings in the bay. Seaward, on the
> crest of a cone-shaped hill, stands the signal pole of the lookout station.

The smoke from the shore stations had to be smelled to be believed. As one contemporary account stated, the smell was "not over grateful to other nostrils than those of born whalers."

Many of the whales caught by shore-based whalers were migrating grays. Since grays migrate along the California coast from December through February and humpback whales from August to December, the two species supported a business that lasted over seven months per year. It is estimated that between 1854 and 1874, over 2,500 whales were taken by shore-based whalers in California. The number of whales that were wounded and escaped to die later is not known. In September 1854, the *Crescent City Herald* described one such loss that took place close in to shore:

> For the space of a quarter of an hour the scene was most exciting, the
> wounded animal now lashed the water in a perfect fury, then darted
> off with the speed of an arrow ... the harpoon parted its hold much to
> the disappointment of the spectators as well as the boat's crew.

In the beginning it was a lucrative business; the average gray whale yielded about thirty-five barrels of oil, and the average humpback about forty to forty-five barrels. By 1865, the price of whale oil had soared to over $45 per barrel, so the profit was substantial. In addition, humpback baleen brought a decent price; gray whale baleen was too short to be of any value. Whale sinews sold for about twenty-five cents per pound; they were usually exported to China, where they were used in soups.

By 1870, eleven shore-based whaling stations existed on the California coast. Ten years later, the gray whale was so scarce that most of the stations were abandoned. The last station to close down was at Monterey, which lasted until about 1900. The shore station at Point Lobos on Carmel Bay has been restored and is now part of Point Lobos State Reserve.

The one-two punch of lagoon whaling and shore whaling severely decimated the gray whale population. In 1866, only forty-one gray whales were taken, and only 160 were spotted migrating off San Simeon, California. By the mid-1870s, only about two thousand to five thousand gray whales were left, less than half the original population. It has been estimated that between 1845 and 1874, over eight thousand gray whales were killed. Scammon predicted in his 1874 book that "ere long it may be questioned whether this mammal will not be numbered among the extinct species of the Pacific." In 1910, naturalist Roy Chapman Andrews declared, "For over twenty years the species has been lost to science and naturalists believe it to be extinct," a vast overstatement, but an accurate reflection of the prevailing opinion.

Much of the success of the early whalers can be attributed to the 1865 invention of the explosive harpoon gun by a New Bedford captain, a huge improvement over both hand-held whale weaponry and bow-mounted muzzle-loaders. In 1868, the Norwegian whaler Sven Foyn improved upon the invention. Foyn added a glass vial of sulfuric acid which broke when the harpoon entered the whale, detonating an explosive charge inside the animal's body. Even though this new cannon was heavy, weighing almost a ton, it soon became the whaling standard, allowing the shooting of whales from over thirty meters (100 feet) feet away. Soon seas around the world were filled with the sounds of harpoon explosions echoing across the waves, and with the gurgly blows of dying whales. In 1880, steam-powered whaling ships were first introduced to the west coast and whaling leaped to a new level of efficiency.

Baleen was still in high demand, its price jumping from $1.02 a pound in 1868 to $2.00 in 1880. By the turn of the century, the price had more than doubled again, to $5.00 a pound. But the development of spring steel soon pushed the price of baleen down, and by 1908, the strong baleen market was a thing of the past.

In addition, around the turn of the century the demand for whale oil dipped badly. Kerosene began to replace whale oil in lamps, and petroleum, a new substance

first discovered in 1859, began to replace whale oil in lubricants, waxes, and polishes. (However, petroleum did not completely replace whale oil as a lubricant until the rapid expansion of the automobile industry in the 1920s and 1930s.) So ingrained was the use of whale oil that many people assumed that petroleum had to be some ancient form of preserved whale oil.

As the inshore whales in Baja and California were depleted, whalers moved north.

Captain Larsen at the harpoon gun on the S.S. Lawrence *whaling ship, circa 1908. (BC Archives: #D-03820)*

Modern whaling in British Columbia began in 1904 with the launching of a steam-powered whaling ship imported from Norway. In 1905, the first whaling station on Vancouver Island was opened, at Sechart in Barkley Sound. It was followed by a station at Kyuquot in 1907 and a winter station at Page's Lagoon in the same year. Two stations were set up in 1911 in the Queen Charlotte Islands: one at Rose Harbour and one at Naden Harbour. In 1948, the last of the BC whaling stations opened at Coal Harbour in Quatsino Sound at the north end of Vancouver Island. Experienced Japanese crews were often used at BC whaling stations to carve up the whales and much of the meat was sent to Japan.

Whaling in British Columbia reached its peak in 1911, when 1,199 whales were caught. Around 1912, large factory whaling ships were developed which could process whales aboard ship, reducing the need for shore-based whaling stations. In 1913, the first factory ship used to hunt gray whales anchored off the coastal lagoons of Baja.

The factory ships used a new type of harpoon with an exploding tip. Upon entering a whale, the tip of a harpoon would explode, springing out iron flukes that prevented the harpoon from easily pulling out of the whale. William A. Hagelund, a young trainee on BC whalers in the early 1900s, described one such kill in his book *Whalers No More*:

> *The whole side of the whale was bulged outwards by the force of that terrible internal explosion, and for a split second the whale froze in shock, his ... spout terminated with a pink froth ... we had hit his lungs ...His flukes lashed the water to a foam ... Fifteen minutes later, his blows dark pink with foaming blood, our whale slowed his pace ... we sheered to starboard across the whale's tail {and shot it again} ... The tremendous explosion ... hid the final moments from our eyes, but ... when the smoke cleared, the whale lay dead.*

Whales that were not immediately hit in a vital spot were often dispatched with hand-held lances. "Usually it took two of us together to plunge a lance down into the whale and twist it around till it broke a vital organ or got into the lungs ... I never did really get used to that," recalled Hagelund.

Dead whales were towed to whaling stations on shore, where winches dragged them up a ramp known as a whaleslip. Huge strips of skin and blubber were cut off the whale with massive flensing knives. The strips were then chopped up into small chunks and put into kettles or cookers to render off the oil. A 1908 development called hydrogenation allowed the oil to be solidified for use in such products as margarine, shortening, soap, lubricants, lipsticks, and face creams. The meat was ground into meat meal for mink and pet food, and the bones were ground up for bone meal. The solid residue left after the oil was boiled off was dried and sold as "dried guano" for fertilizer. Even the milk from female whales was condensed and sold.

The bones of about 400 whales at the Sechart Whaling Station in Barkley Sound, British Columbia, circa 1905.
(BC Archives: #D-03824)

Despite strong marketing efforts and testimonials describing it as "looking like strips of tenderloin beef," whale meat never caught on as human fare in North America. In Japan, however, the fishy-tasting meat was very popular and pickled whale tails from British Columbia were often sent to Japan.

Between 1911 and 1913, over four thousand whales were caught off the BC coast and the glut of whale oil temporarily depressed the market. By 1920, the west coast of North America produced one-tenth of the total world production of whale oil.

During the depression years, world consumption of margarine increased dramatically and the demand for whale oil increased along with it. Over eighty percent of the world production of whale oil was used for margarine during this period. In 1925, a record 133 gray whales were killed for their oil, the highest one-year harvest since the bad old days of Baja lagoon whaling. In the winter of 1924-1925 and again in 1928-1929, history repeated itself, and Norwegian and American factory ships hunted gray whales once again along the Baja coast. The Norwegian ships alone took 182 gray whales off Baja between 1925 and 1929.

Despite the huge numbers of whales that were being taken, industrialists refused to believe that the world whale populations were being decimated. In 1928, a report for Lever Brothers, a manufacturer of soaps and a major consumer of whale oil, declared: "The view held in all well-informed quarters was there was no likelihood of a shortage of whales generally." This attitude led to an overproduction of whale oil, whose price dropped in 1934 to less than half its 1929 price.

But in the field, more and more whalers were reporting that their targets were becoming harder and harder to find. The League of Nations tried to effect international controls in 1930, modeled after Norway's whaling laws, but nobody paid attention. In 1931, the Geneva Convention for the Regulation of Whaling was signed by twenty-six nations and became effective in 1935. Germany, Japan, and the Soviet Union refused to sign. Even these early controls did not go far enough, however, so a new International Agreement for the Regulation of Whaling was signed in London in 1937. Article 4 of the Agreement stated, "It is forbidden to take or kill grey-whales." However, due to a lack of enforcement and the refusal of many nations (especially Japan and the Soviet Union) to honor the agreement, between 1937 and 1938 a record 55,000 whales of all species were caught, the highest catch prior to World War II. In terms of tonnage, the 1938 catch was the largest catch ever.

Although no accurate census was taken, it is believed that the gray whale population again dropped to very low levels after the 1930s. By the end of that decade, the bowhead whale was becoming very scarce, and many aboriginal hunters on the Chukotka Peninsula of Asia switched to hunting grays. In 1937, Russian biologist B.A. Zenkovich warned, "We are dealing with a rapidly disappearing species." By 1938, one biologist estimated that only about two hundred gray whales existed. Another went so far as to declare the species extinct.

By 1941, baleen, once the most valuable part of a whale, had dropped in value to less than five cents a pound, and was dumped into deep water as garbage. Whale meat became the most valuable part of the whale.

During World War II, the whale hunt took a brief rest as whaling ships were altered for use as oil tankers. But as soon as the war ended, there was a huge demand for fats and oils, and whalers readied their ships for a renewed attack on the world's whales. The war years also produced two new technological spin-offs in the form of surplus helicopters and airplanes, which were increasingly used to spot whales from the air.

Recognizing the threat to the world's whales, the United States government convened a meeting in Washington, DC, in the fall of 1946. After two weeks of negotiations, the conference announced the formation of the International Whaling Commission (IWC). US Secretary of State Dean Acheson declared: "The world's whale stocks are a truly international resource in that they belong to no single nation, not to a group of nations, but rather they are the wards of the entire world."

As foster parents of the world's whales, the IWC failed miserably. Torn apart by internal disputes and commercial greed, the IWC did not call its first meeting until 1949. It has had a spotty record since then, primarily due to the failure of Japan, Iceland, Norway, and the Soviet Union to honor the rules set out by the commission. During the first thirty years of the IWC's existence, an appalling 1.5 million whales were caught and killed by commercial whalers. Between 1938 and 1947, one Soviet factory ship alone, the *Aleut*, killed 471 gray whales.

However, almost alone among the various species of whales in the world, the gray whale was bouncing back. In December 1946, a biologist studying marine birds near Point Loma, California, spotted a few gray whales. Upon hearing about the whales, Carl L. Hubbs of the Scripps Institute of Oceanography flew over the Baja lagoons in a Coast Guard plane and noted "rather many gray whales." He then "conducted a routine census of the migrating whales, first from the roof of a Scripps building, with powerful binoculars, and later from a plane covering the whole breeding range of the gray whale." His efforts confirmed that the gray whale was slowly rebuilding itself to old levels.

One of the most contentious clauses of the 1946 controls on whaling allowed the taking of gray whales by aboriginal groups, stating "the taking of gray whales in the Bering and Chukchi seas should be permitted when the meat and products of such whales are to be used for local consumption by the aborigines of the Chukotsk and Korjaksk areas." Alaskan Eskimos used this clause to take only one or two grays a year, but the Soviets were another matter.

Until 1955, the catch by Siberian Chukchi Natives varied from two to thirty whales a year. However, after 1955 it suddenly soared to nearly two hundred a year. Conservationists did a bit of math and found that unless the aboriginal population of the Chukchi Sea area had suddenly boomed, the average family in the area would have to eat about ten tons of whale meat a year to use up the two hundred whales. When queried, the Soviets argued that to make the hunt more efficient, they hunted whales for the aboriginal people with a huge catcher boat called the *Zevezdny*. Conservationists suspected that the Soviets were illegally catching grays for commercial purposes, but were unable to gather proof.

In 1959, the Soviet Union again defied the IWC by announcing plans to quadruple the size of their fleet of whaling ships, two of which were 36,000 gross tonnes (33,000 gross tons) in weight, the largest whaling whips ever built.

Another exemptive clause in the IWC regulations allowed the taking of gray whales for scientific purposes. In Canada, ten gray whales were killed in 1953 under a special scientific permit and taken to Coal Harbour on Vancouver Island for dissection.

World whaling reached its peak in the 1960s. The highest one-year catch of whales ever recorded was in 1961, when 66,090 whales were killed. In 1962, Tokyo's Taiyo Gogyo Company, the world's largest fishing company, entered into partnership with BC Packers to hunt whales off the BC coast.

But by the 1960s, the world suddenly realized that its resources were not endless. In the words of veteran whale biologist Victor Scheffer, "There was a national self-examination, a kind of cultural revolution almost as important as the Industrial Revolution." And there was no better symbol for the rape of the world than the decrease in the world whale populations.

Ironically, just as the world was awakening to the plight of the world's whales, American biologists took advantage of the IWC loophole allowing the taking of whales for scientific purposes. Between 1959 and 1969, 316 gray whales, seventy-seven of which were pregnant females, were killed by catcher boats for Dale W. Rice and Allen A. Wolman, then with the Bureau of Commercial Fisheries in Seattle. Rice and Wolman were frank in the reasoning for the slaughter: "The California gray whale stock has increased so much that a resumption of commercial exploitation has been considered." In hindsight, it is hard to believe that the government could have been so blind to the sweeping environmental movement that boomed in the 1960s, but then tunnel vision has always been a common ailment among bureaucrats.

The two researchers dissected and measured the dead whales at a shore-based whaling station, and produced a 142-page study that did provide a wealth of gray whale data. Strangely, the report was entitled "The Life History and Ecology of the Gray Whale," although no life history for the gray whale was given. Even though the study estimated the late 1960s population of gray whales at around 11,000, politics and the environmental movement intervened and prevented the resumption of the gray whale hunt.

In 1969, Greenpeace was formed. The British Columbia-based group was originally founded to oppose nuclear testing in the Aleutians and South Pacific, but soon turned into the strongest anti-whaling voice in the world. "Save the Whale" became the rallying call of the 1970s. In 1970, the United States added eight whale species to those listed in the Endangered Species Act. One of the eight was the California gray whale.

Forced by a lack of demand for whale products and the pressures of conservationists, most nations slowly eased out of the whaling business. Canada's last whaling station, Coal Harbour, closed its doors for good in 1967, due to a lack of the big meat-producing whales: blue, fin, and sei whales. In the United States, the last whaling station was the Del Monte Fishing Company station in Richmond, California. It did not close its doors until 1971.

By 1972, Jacques Cousteau joyfully declared that "man has become convinced ... that the whale is the greatest and most intriguing of nature's marine mammals, the most stupendous form of animal life in the seas." That same year, the UN Conference on the Human Environment called for a ten-year moratorium on all commercial whaling. Both the United States and Canada stopped whaling as a result of the call, but the idea was rejected by the majority of IWC members.

Jacques Cousteau declared in 1972 that the whale was "the greatest and most intriguing of nature's marine mammals." (Institut Oceanographique, Monaco)

The Russian whaling ship Vladivostock *reeling in one of its kills, 1976.* (Rex Weyler/ Greenpeace)

In the meantime the gray whale population was slowly recovering. By 1975, the population had recovered to about 10,000 to 15,000 individuals, an amazing comeback from the brink of extinction. In 1978, the IWC dropped its protection of the California gray whale, changing its status from a "Protected Stock" to a "Sustained Management Stock" with an allowed catch of 178 per year. In 1992, the gray whale became the first marine mammal to be downlisted from endangered to threatened status. In 1994, it was removed from the threatened and endangered list altogether.

During this same period, the mystery of the high Soviet harvest of gray whales was solved. In 1981 eco-warrior Paul Watson finally infiltrated the Soviet whaling station of Loren on the Siberian coast and was shocked by what he saw:

> *Piles of fresh whale meat littered the area with some very unaboriginal-type women employed … We were close enough to see their blondish hair … and blue eyes. So much for the aboriginal justification for the hunt. The meat was transported up the slope to a small warehouse … bordered by … sheds. We could plainly see that the sheds were shelters for what were obviously cages. We were looking at a mink ranch. This so-called aboriginal hunt was nothing more than a front for a commercial mink farm.*

The IWC anti-whaling moratorium motion did not pass until 1982, becoming effective in 1986. The Soviet Union finally stopped commercial whaling the next year. Today, only Japan and Korea continue to ignore the whaling moratorium, with the result that the gray whale off their shores is almost extinct.

The gray whale off North American shores is in much better shape, with an estimated current population of about 20,000 to 25,000 whales, which probably equals the original population before its exploitation by humans. The only gray whales legally taken today are those caught by aboriginals in Alaska and the Russian Republic.

The IWC catch limit for California gray whales, which may be taken by or on behalf of aboriginal peoples, is 124 per year; the catch reported for 1995 was eighty-five.

Recently, a new threat has appeared on the horizon, with the formation of the World Council of Whalers, a group led by Japan and Norway that promotes the revival of whaling by Natives around the world. In 1997, the Nuu-Chah-Nulth people of Vancouver Island (formerly the Nootka nation) announced that they wished to resume the hunt for gray whales with the aid of Japanese and Norwegian commercial whalers. Most of the Nuu-Chah-Nulth people, however, disclaimed the announcement, calling it "nothing but a political move." The announcement brought calls of outrage from conservationists, who called it "a giant step backward."

In June 1997, Japan and Norway filed a proposal to the 138-member Convention on International Trade in Endangered Species (CITES) to resume the whaling of various whale species which they say are abundant. The two countries failed to win the necessary two-thirds majority for their proposal and it was defeated. In the words of one CITES member, "as long as there is human greed, there will always be human pressure on whales."

In October 1997, the IWC granted permission for Washington State's Makah Native tribe to kill four gray whales per year. Conservationists have vowed to sue to stop the hunt, stating that the proposed use of high-powered rifles hardly qualifies as a traditional native hunting method.

Closeup of the steel tip of a whaling harpoon. (Robert H. Busch/ Artifact courtesy The Whale Centre, Tofino, BC)

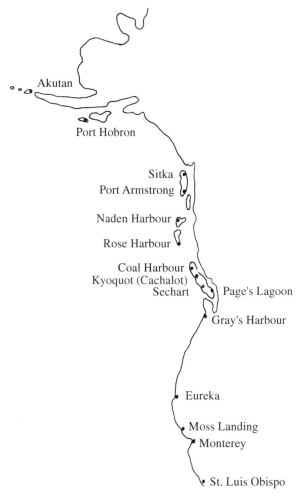

Akutan

Port Hobron

Sitka
Port Armstrong

Naden Harbour

Rose Harbour

Coal Harbour
Kyoquot (Cachalot)
Sechart   Page's Lagoon

Gray's Harbour

Eureka

Moss Landing
Monterey

St. Luis Obispo

Whaling centres of North America,
1900–1971.

Whale-watching

The migration of the gray whale close to the North American coast presents an unequaled opportunity for whale-watching. It is estimated that over two million people along the west coast of North America watch the gray whales each year. In San Diego alone, over 300,000 people a year watch the whales on their annual trek. Other popular whale-watching spots in the United States include Yaquina Head, north of Newport, Oregon, and Yankee Point, south of Monterey, California.

The American whale-watching industry began in San Diego in 1955, when a single boat went out to show tourists gray whales. The first tour boat entered Scammon's Lagoon in 1970. Today, over three hundred whale-watching boats leave the California coast every year to watch grays in state or Mexican waters. It is estimated that North America's gray whale-watching industry brings in over $10 million every year, easily exceeding the income once produced from the killing of grays.

In Canada, the area around Pacific Rim National Park on the west coast of Vancouver Island is prime whale-watching territory. Gray whales migrate past the Park between February and late May, peaking in the last two weeks of March. In addition, a summer population of about thirty-five to fifty gray whales reside in the area from May through November. Just south of the Park lies the town of Ucluelet. Ucluelet is an Indian word meaning "safe harbor" or "people with a safe landing place." In recent years, it has grandly dubbed itself the "Whale-Watching Capital of the World," a fancy title for a little fishing village. To the north of the Park lies the charming town of Tofino, one of the first spots in Canada visited by Captain Cook. Tofino is a popular tourist destination, with trendy art galleries and excellent restaurants. The town sits at the entrance to Clayoquot Sound, one of the most spectacular coastal inlets in Canada and the past site of heated demonstrations opposing the runaway clearcutting that has destroyed so much of British Columbia's coastal rainforests. Both towns depend heavily upon tourist dollars brought in by whale-watchers and use the whale as a sign of civic pride. In Tofino there is a Whale Song Gallery, a Whale Centre, and a Coffee Pod cafe, which features a Gray Whale blend of coffee. Ucluelet has a Gray Whale Deli, a Whale's Tale Restaurant, and Mo-B-Dick Video Rentals. A dozen companies in the Ucluelet-Tofino area offer excellent whale-watching tours.

The tour companies in Tofino seem to be especially well managed and courteous. There is no cutthroat competition for the tourists' dollars, as in other spots on the western coast, and the tour-boat drivers show great respect for the whales. Most of the paying passengers also show a genuine respect for the whales and the need to keep a safe distance, although I met one brain-dead tourist who couldn't understand why we couldn't get closer to the whales. Many of the tour companies in Tofino donate a portion of their income to whale research, making the tour especially worthwhile. Most of the tourists who come to the Ucluelet-Tofino area are thrilled just to spot a gray whale, but some come expecting a bit more.

According to biologist Jim Darling, "whales have proven to be incredibly tolerant of people." Tofino-based whale researcher Rod Palm tells a story about the time he was filming a gray whale underwater: "The whale looked right into the camera," he says, "then turned around and gently pushed the camera away with its tail."

Occasionally, the tolerance of grays for humans goes one step farther. Although the majority of grays ignore or avoid humans, in recent years the phenomenon of unusually friendly gray whales has developed, attracting tourists who hope to do more than just see a distant whale spout or a mighty tail disappearing into the depths.

The phenomenon was first documented in the early 1960s, when "curious and friendly whales" were encountered in San Ignacio Lagoon. In 1975, a gray whale in San Ignacio Lagoon lost its fear of the tourist boats in the Baja lagoons and rubbed against them. Biologists interpreted the action as a simple means of rubbing off pesky

A boat dock at Tofino, British Columbia, at the entrance to spectacular Clayoquot Sound. (Robert H. Busch)

barnacles and lice, and thought it was an isolated phenomenon.

In 1976, a juvenile whale named George began delighting tourists to San Ignacio Lagoon when he batted around small skiffs tied behind the tourist boats. Again, biologists believed that George was either rubbing off parasites or enjoyed the feel of the skiffs against his skin. Pachico Mayoral, a San Ignacio fisherman, believed the actions represented true friendliness, saying, "One reason for their friendliness may be this lagoon's small community. There have been so few people here to bother the whales."

But then in 1978, a Baja tourist stretched out a broom and scratched a gray whale that was loafing near a tourist boat. The whale seemed to like it, leaning into the broom and then presenting its other side to be scratched. According to biologist Roger Payne, "The following year there were two or three whales behaving this way, and something like six or eight the year after, until the news apparently spread among the whales that boats were safe and even offered pleasant contact." He called the fearless whales "friendlies," echoing the label that Mexican fishermen use: *ballenas amistosas*, or "friendly whales."

In the mid-1980s, the whales began to be more insistent, pushing hard against the boats and soliciting pets and rubs from the delighted tourists aboard. Biologists were surprised at the lack of fear on the part of the whales, for no other whale species is known to allow so much human contact. Tourists flocked to the Baja lagoons, many of them eager to actually touch a living gray whale, and going home terribly disappointed if they didn't.

In 1982, biologists Mary Lou Jones and Steve Swartz had encounters with "at least 200 friendly whales" in San Ignacio Lagoon. They reported "frequent approaches to skiffs from astern as though curious about the source of the engine sound."

Friendly gray whales are often encountered in whale-watching tours to the Baja lagoons.
(Ken Jacques/Baja Expeditions)

The friendly whale phenomenon is not limited to the whales in the Baja lagoons, and has been documented from Baja right up to the Arctic. In 1982, one researcher in the Bering Sea reported that he was followed for about twenty minutes by a friendly gray whale.

In British Columbia, Jim Darling was once phoned by a policeman who complained that a gray whale had rammed his boat. "We're going to have to destroy it," the policeman said. Darling asked if the whale had rolled over onto its back after ramming the boat. "Well, yes," the policeman said. "As a matter of fact it did." And Darling replied, "Well, scratch its belly, that's what it wants."

Unfortunately, there are always a few members of the human species who destroy such unique encounters due to ignorance. In 1982, one friendly whale showed up at Tofino and spent several weeks in the area. Then an ignorant local resident went out in a boat and lifted his dog onto the whale's back. When the terrified dog bit the whale, it dove, and when it resurfaced, the man drove his boat over the whale's back, slashing deep cuts into the skin. The whale quickly swam away and not surprisingly has never returned.

Due to the sheer size of the gray whale, it is inevitable that some accidents have occurred between whales and humans who get too close to them. In 1968, a gray whale came up for air under a Zodiac holding three of Jacques Cousteau's divers, accidentally dumping all three into the water. In the late 1970s, one gray came up under a boat in San Ignacio Lagoon, breaking the floorboards and dumping the people in the boat into the warm water. In 1982, a whale in Scammon's Lagoon upset a small boat, drowning two people. One kayaker got too close to a calf and was rammed by its mother, fortunately without serious injury to whale or human. And a helicopter hovering far too close to the water's surface was drenched by the huge splash of a whale's tail, lost power, and barely made it to shore.

Another accident occurred when Howard Hall was filming gray whales in San Ignacio Lagoon and had a close encounter of the worst kind. As Hall reported in *International Wildlife* magazine, one whale swam close to him, and then:

A friendly gray whale enjoys a close encounter with humans on the west coast of Vancouver Island. (Richard Beaupied/The Whale Centre, Tofino, BC)

The whale quickly turned and accelerated away ... Then the impact came ... At my left side I caught the fleeting image of the flukes as they smashed into my body, edge on. In my head, I heard the sound of an explosion as if a shotgun had been fired in my ear. Then the lights went out.

Hall emerged from his accident with two broken ribs and a fractured arm.

Incidents such as these prove how important it is that a proper distance be kept between gray whales and humans. Commercial tour boats today generally show common sense in approaching gray whales, for adverse reactions from the whales would jeopardize their business.

In Canada, the Department of Fisheries and Oceans has expressed concerns "that uncontrolled whale-watching will harm or displace whales that inhabit or migrate through Canadian coastal waters." The Department has established informal whale-watching guidelines which recommend that whale-watching aircraft stay a minimum of three hundred meters (1,000 feet) above the water's surface and that boats stay at least 100 meters (300 feet) away from a whale. Most tour boats respect these guidelines, but on a recent trip to Tofino I did find one tour boat driver who incorrectly believed that the guidelines applied only to killer whales and not to grays, "because gray whales are no longer endangered."

It is also recommended that boats near to whales shut off their engines, for the sound of a small outboard motor is very similar to the low frequency sounds made by gray whales and often attracts them. Biologist Steve Swartz found that "if we shut the engine off, the friendlies would leave the boat, abandon it."

Today, in the San Ignacio Lagoon, boats are no longer allowed in the middle and upper portions of the lagoon, and are only allowed in the lower lagoon with a special permit. Such precautions help ensure that future generations of both humans and whales can enjoy each other's company for years to come.

Gray Whales in Captivity

Gray whales have been kept in captivity on only three occasions, all at Sea World in San Diego. In 1965, Sea World hired a Japanese gunner who harpooned a baby gray whale in Scammon's Lagoon. The injured whale, crippled by a collapsed lung, was quickly shipped to Sea World, where it only survived for two months.

In 1971, Sea World tried again. A team succeeded in lassoing a two-month-old five-meter (18-foot) calf, whose frantic mother repeatedly attacked and slightly damaged the catcher ship before giving up and swimming away. The calf was taken to Sea World, where it refused to eat for the first two weeks and lost sixty eight kilograms (150 pounds). Finally, it was force-fed a gooey mix of cream, ground squid and fish, cod-liver oil, yeast, vitamins, and water. Later the calf, named Gigi by the aquarium staff, took larger squid and fish by sucking them off the floor of its tank.

Gigi was the subject of many scientific tests; she was weighed, measured, her respiration and heart rate was taken, and blood and feces samples were obtained for analysis. She was found to weigh 1,950 kilograms (4,300 pounds), and grew fast. So fast, in fact, that Sea World was soon spending $200 a day on food for her.

One day, Bud Donahoo, her keeper, accidentally sprayed water on her flukes while cleaning out her tank. To his amazement, she lifted them up and held them in the spray, obviously enjoying the feeling. This led to him rubbing her and establishing a series of hand pats as signals: one pat for "pay attention," two for "open your mouth," and three for "no" or "settle down." Donahoo was amazed, and stated, "I believe that this animal can be communicated with by sound." To his regret, biologists ignored his discovery, believing it to be unnatural behavior created by captivity.

Soon Gigi had outgrown her tank and was moved to a fifteen-meter (50-foot) circular tank, where she spent a lot of time lying at the bottom of the tank near the water inlet. She was given a bottlenose dolphin for company, and the two played together as much as the limited room allowed. Finally Gigi grew too large to be kept in captivity. Before being released back to the wild, Gigi was freeze-branded with a 0.6-meter (2-foot)-square white mark for future identification. In addition, a radio-transmitter was surgically attached to her back with nylon sutures. By this time, Gigi weighed over 6,000 kilograms (14,000 pounds) and was over eight meters (26 feet) long.

In March 1972, she was released off the California coast, almost exactly one year after capture. Gigi spent her first hours swimming in circles, apparently confused by the lack of tank walls. She vocalized strongly, giving out over 1,300 clicks in four minutes, a sound that she had never used in captivity. Then she slowly began to swim north, following the ancient urge to migrate northward in the spring. She was tracked by biologist William Evans of the Naval Undersea Center, but her transmitter worked only when its antenna was above water, and Evans frequently lost track of her. The transmitter worked for the last time near Monterey on May 5, 1972.

Since then, Gigi has been sighted many times, although some of the sightings are a bit doubtful. One of the first sightings was in January, 1973 near San Diego. Then in January 1974, one of her trainers was giving a lecture on a whale-watching boat and believes she spotted Gigi, basing her identification on a scar on the lower part of the whale's body. In February 1975, Gigi was reportedly spotted in Scammon's Lagoon. A boater off San Diego's Point Loma spotted her in December 1977 and took her picture. In 1979, she was seen in San Ignacio Lagoon, reportedly with a calf at her side. In 1972, a year after Gigi's release, the US government passed the Marine Mammal Protection Act, making it illegal for whales of any type to be captured for use as aquarium exhibits without a special permit.

Such special permission was given in 1997 in the rescue of an abandoned gray whale calf found thrashing in the shallows off the California coast. The calf was just a few days old, with its umbilical cord still attached. It was taken to Sea World, where it was found to be dehydrated, nearly comatose, and barely alive. It was placed into a 545,000-liter (120,000-gallon) pool and given antibiotics, fluids, and nutritious food. The whale barely moved for the first few hours, then finally opened her eyes and began her struggle for survival. The calf, dubbed J.J., gained more than 0.5 kilograms (1 pound) per hour in her first few days, and hopefully will be released off the California coast in the winter to rejoin the migrating grays.

Although it is unlikely that a gray whale will ever again be kept in captivity, except for rescue and rehabilitation cases, the story of Gigi calls into question the whole debate over whales in captivity. Desmond Morris, the ex-curator of animals at Regent's Park Zoo in London, and the famed author of *The Naked Ape*, made headlines in 1968 with this statement: "There is something biologically immoral about keeping animals in enclosures where their behavior patterns, which have taken millions of years to evolve, can find no expression."

Most humane societies today use a general rule of thumb that to provide proper room for exercise, the enclosure for any species should have a minimum length of ten times the body length of the animal. This means that for an adult gray whale, an aquarium pool would have to be at least 106 to 137 meters (350 to 450 feet) in diameter, many times the size of most aquarium pools.

Nevertheless, the only way that many people will ever see a number of wild species is within the confines of aquariums and zoos, and there is no question that an educational value exists. In addition, as the case of Gigi showed, many biological observations and measurements can only be taken in a captive setting, and ultimately the management of many species depends on the accumulation of this kind of data.

For most people, as long as the enclosure is large enough (which is almost impossible for adult gray whales) and the animals' physical and mental needs are provided for, the keeping of most animals in captivity is acceptable. The problem is that many zoos and aquariums are third-rate facilities in which animals suffer in small cages, with no toys or pastimes provided to prevent stress and boredom. I'll never forget seeing an orangutan sitting in a concrete cage in a well-known zoo, with nothing to climb on, nothing to play with, and no companions to interact with. The poor animal was just sitting there, pulling out his hair for a lack of anything else to do. If we must keep animals in captivity, it is our responsibility to do so humanely. I can only hope that cities, towns, counties, and states will someday wake up and enact legislation to prevent the suffering of animals in third-rate facilities. Our fellow animals deserve better.

The Ballad of Bonnet and Crossbeak

Although most gray whales depart Arctic waters before they are covered with an impenetrable sheet of ice, occasionally a few whales remain too long and pay for the incident with their lives.

In the fall of 1988, three gray whales near Point Barrow, Alaska, almost joined the list of the departed. Eskimo hunters found the three trapped in the ice, with only a small breathing hole left open to keep them alive. Word of the three trapped whales soon reached the outside world, where it became an international news story. Conservationists, journalists, and aboriginals joined forces to save the three whales by cutting holes in the ice with chainsaws. A hover barge blasted warm compressed air over the main breathing hole to help keep it open, and a skycrane pounded a series of holes through the ice with a 5.5-tonne (5-ton) hammer. The whole operation was dubbed Operation Breakthrough. Even President Reagan got into the act, piously announcing to the press that he was praying for the whales.

The whales, however, were hesitant to leave their breathing hole, and refused to swim over to the newly cut holes. At one point it seemed that the whales were about to move off in the right direction, but when all the reporters and photographers rushed over to the ice in front of them, they held back. Soon the jagged ice had cut their sensitive skins, and drips of red blood tainted the pristine white landscape.

A gray whale trapped in the ice in Alaska in 1988 takes a good look at his icy prison. (François Gohier)

Despite all the heroic efforts, the smallest of the whales—known as Bone, for it had scraped all the flesh off its snout—died, and sank beneath the water's surface. The young whale, estimated to have been about nine months old, was simply too weak to survive the traumatic incident. The remaining duo were dubbed Bonnet and Crossbeak, the former for a barnacle patch on its head, and the latter for its distorted mouth, which did not close properly. Finally a Soviet icebreaker, the *Admiral Makarov*, sliced a channel through the ice leading to open water, and on October 28, the two lucky whales swam away to freedom.

The 1988 entrapment of three gray whales in Alaska became an international news item.
(François Gohier)

Most of the world celebrated the rescue, but Great Britain's Prince Philip put his royal foot in his mouth when he issued a statement condemning the vast expense "wasted" on the three whales. (The rescue was estimated to have cost just over a million dollars.) Hundreds of angry responses were sent to Buckingham Palace, many of them pointing out that as honorary chairman of the World Wildlife Fund, Philip should have had more compassion.

Despite the blue-blood's blunder, the incident points out just how far human-kind has come in the past hundred years, from hunting the gray whale to the point of extinction to doing everything in our power to save three stranded individuals. It is incidents like these that give me hope for the future of the world's whales.

Chapter Four   To Save a Species

If we survive, we will care for whales and the other wild creatures and if we perish through our own cleverness, the end of the wild things will have been an early warning of our folly.
— Victor Scheffer, whale biologist, 1974

For three years, I lived on a remote acreage in the mountains of central British Columbia, where I kept a tally of the animals I saw each year. The first winter I was there, I counted nineteen moose over the winter. The next year I only counted eleven. The following year there were five, and in my last year there were only two. The dual threats of habitat loss due to clearcutting and overhunting each fall had a marked effect on the moose population. If I could notice the results in my little valley, I couldn't even imagine what was happening over the whole province.

The same principles involved in the moose decimation apply to whales and all other wild creatures. In order for whales to thrive the world over, we must first understand their biological needs and then enact efficient management programs to conserve them.

Whale Research

In the past twenty years whale research has become a crowded field, as more and more biologists aim their sights on the vast expanse of ocean that covers planet Earth. Their task is not to be taken lightly, for the romance of working with the largest animals on Earth soon cools under the conditions in which whale researchers often work: rocky seas, frigid water, and a permanent state of underfunding.

In the world of gray whale research, three names continually pop up in the literature: Mary Lou Jones, Steve Swartz, and Jim Darling. Jones and Swartz work

FACING PAGE: *This carcass of a gray whale was found beside the San Ignacio Lagoon in Baja, site of pioneer research by Mary Lou Jones and Steve Swartz.* (Frank S. Balthis/Nature's Design)

out of California, and performed pioneer field work in Baja California. Jim Darling is Canada's most respected gray whale expert, and is based in Tofino, British Columbia.

Jones & Swartz: At Play in the Fields of the Whale

Steve Swartz received a bachelor's degree from the University of California at Santa Barbara and began working on his master's degree in ichthyology. However, when an interesting job came along teaching students who visited Sea World in San Diego, Swartz jumped at the chance. At Sea World, Swartz met Mary Lou Jones, a trainer who shared his interest in marine mammals. Both were members of the American Cetacean Society and volunteered for its annual San Diego winter gray whale census.

This led to the idea of an intensive research project observing gray whales in one of Baja California's calving lagoons. They formed Cetacean Research Associates, and with the financial backing of the National Geographic Society, the World Wildlife Fund, the Marine Mammal Commission, and others, they began recording gray whale behavior in San Ignacio Lagoon.

At the time, Scammon's Lagoon was the spot that tourists headed to, and San Ignacio Lagoon was one of the least visited of the calving lagoons, making it a good spot for observations. "We wanted to look at whales without the influence of humans around," says Swartz. And at twenty-five kilometers (17 miles) long and only three kilometers (2 miles) wide, the lagoon is small enough to be easily surveyed by two people.

From 1977 through 1982, the two set up camp on Punta Piedra (Rocky Point), a peninsula at the mouth of the lagoon. "It was surrounded on three sides by impenetrable mangrove estuary, so you were, in fact, on an island," says Swartz. The local ravens were delighted to find new intruders to pester: "They'd turn over our stoves, empty trash bins, tear open bags, and scatter things around. They were quite hilarious," recalls Swartz.

Not quite so funny were the gale-force winds which swept across the area. The winds, known as *chubascos*, tore down tents and made life more than miserable. "We had a Super Cub there one season and it tried to fly by itself," says Swartz. "We had to chain it to the ground." They set up a viewing tower on four-and-a-half-meter (15-foot) aluminum legs and recorded many hours of first-time gray whale observations. Many of the whales were given names like Peanut, Pinto, Rosebud, and Bopper. The last was named for his habit of "coming up under the boat and giving it a good whack," says Swartz.

Another whale, named Amazing Grace, was much more gentle. Grace, a young female about two years old, was unusually calm and graceful. "From our first encounter with Amazing Grace, she readily adopted us," says Jones. "She would roll under the boat, turn belly up with her flipper sticking three or four feet out of the water on either side of the craft, then lift us clear off the surface of the lagoon, perched high and dry on her chest." Grace also enjoyed much closer human contact. "[She] would often lie quietly alongside the boat to be rubbed," says Jones. "We would oblige her with a vigorous massage along her back and head."

Their five years of field study resulted in a mass of data on gray whale behavior and reproduction, which they used in a number of magazine articles. In 1984, Jones and Swartz, along with Stephen Leatherwood, edited a thick academic book on gray whales entitled *The Gray Whale: Eschrichtius robustus*. That same year, Jones wrote her Master of Science thesis at the Moss Landing Marine Mammal Laboratory, entitled "Gray whale reproduction, distribution, and duration of stay in Laguna San Ignacio, and inter-lagoon exchange of whales in the winter range." The five-year study by Jones and Swartz is now considered one of the pioneering foundations of gray whale biology. Much of the data they collected is still being used today.

Jim Darling: From Surfer to Scientist

Dr. James D. Darling began his career as a surfer in the 1960s at Long Beach, an eleven-kilometer (7 mile) stretch of surf-swept sand on the west coast of Vancouver Island. "I would be getting ready for a ride when gray whales … would blow a few feet away," he says. "It always came close to stopping my heart."

Long Beach, the seven-mile stretch of sand off which Jim Darling began his gray whale research.
(Robert H. Busch)

These chance meetings led to a lifelong career. When Long Beach became part of Pacific Rim National Park in 1971, Darling took a summer job driving a tour boat. "The idea was to make money for school and do a bunch of surfing in between," he says. His first brush with gray whale science came after graduating in 1972 with a marine biology degree from the University of Victoria, when the superintendent of Pacific Rim National Park paid him to do a literature review on the gray whale.

In 1973 and 1974, he worked as a park naturalist, and took numerous photos of the gray whales which frequented the area. In a 1971 paper, US fisheries biologists

Dale W. Rice and Allen A. Wolman stated, "Individual [gray] whales cannot be observed repeatedly," but by 1973, Darling was doing just that. A lucky meeting with biologist David Hatler confirmed that some of the gray whales were repeatedly sighted year after year feeding in the same general area off Vancouver Island. This led to a joint 1974 paper on this previously undocumented fact of gray whale life.

At a 1975 whale conference in Bloomington, Indiana, Darling met Roger Payne, who was using photo-identification techniques to catalog whales. Afer taking over four thousand photos himself, Darling found that between thirty-five and fifty grays dropped out of the northward migration and spent the summer off Long Beach, rejoining the southward migration in the fall. His research resulted in a 1978 master's thesis entitled "Aspects of the Behavior and Ecology of the Vancouver Island Gray Whales."

Darling's emphasis on gray whales took a short detour when Roger Payne asked him to help work on humpback whales in Hawaii. Darling says he "thought about it for at least five seconds." He spent the next two years helping Payne. In 1980, Darling founded the West Coast Whale Research Foundation as a vehicle for whale research. During his work with Roger Payne, Darling met renowned underwater photographer Flip Nicklin, who convinced him to drop his plan to do a Ph.D. on gray whales in Mexico and study humpback whales in Hawaii instead. This work led to a 1983 Ph.D. written at the University of California at Santa Cruz entitled "Migration, Abundance, and Behavior of Hawaiian Humpback Whales." In 1991, he became part of the Clayoquot Biosphere Project, "a community-based research and education society," where he still serves as Research Director. Currently, Darling is researching both gray whales and humpbacks, the only two large whale species regularly found off the BC coast.

His gray whale work has focused recently on feeding behavior and DNA studies to determine familial relationships. The new technology at his fingertips is a long way from the old black and white photography that marked his entry into the world of the whale. "Times and techniques have changed," he says, "and we have learned more about living whales in their natural environment in the last two decades than in generations of previous efforts."

Whale Management

As a migratory species, the gray whale falls under the legal jurisdiction of three countries: Mexico, the United States, and Canada. Each, to its credit, has taken steps to manage and conserve the gray whales that annually pass by its shores.

Mexico preserved Scammon's Lagoon and the adjacent Guerrero Negro Lagoon as natural reserves in 1972, requiring all commercial vessels, both domestic and foreign, to obtain permits before entering the lagoons. Since 1974, all vessels entering Scammon's Lagoon have had to obtain a permit and are restricted to one lower channel, in order to prevent disturbing the pregnant females in the upper lagoons. Mexico added protection to San Ignacio Lagoon and Magdalena Bay in 1979. Boats are not allowed in either without permission, and in San Ignacio Lagoon, the upper and middle portions of the lagoon are completely off limits to boats between December 15 and March 15 each year. There are limits on the number of tour boats in the lagoon at one time and the number of days that each can remain.

The area around Scammon's Lagoon is now the Parque Naturel de Ballena Gris, or Gray Whale National Park, the first national park in the world created to preserve gray whales. The park is part of the huge 2.4 million-hectare (6 million-acre) Vizcaino Biosphere Reserve, which stretches right across Baja to the Gulf of California. Mexico's three-hundred-kilometer (200-mile) offshore economic zone protects the grays from ever again being harvested offshore by whalers.

In 1972, the United States passed the Marine Mammal Protection Act, which bans the import and killing of whales and most other marine mammals. In 1976, the Fish Conservation and Management Act was added to the lawbooks, extending the US Conservation Zone to three hundred kilometers (200 miles) from shore, effectively protecting the inshore migratory routes of the gray whale. In 1992, 530 kilometers (350 miles) of California coast were designated as the Monterey Bay National Marine Sanctuary, a preserve for seven types of whales, including grays. With these three acts, both the habitat and the future of the gray whale are well protected in the United States.

In Canada, the Fisheries Act of 1868 gave the federal government jurisdiction over the adjacent ocean and its resources. The Whaling Convention Act of 1951 added regulations for the whaling industry, which still existed at that time. Vancouver Island's Pacific Rim National Park was created in 1971. It extends about three kilometers (2 miles) offshore, preserving a thirty-kilometer (20-mile) stretch of summer feeding grounds for gray whales. Canada's offshore economic zone was extended from eighteen kilometers (12 miles) to three hundred kilometers (200 miles) in 1977, giving more than adequate protection for the gray whales' feeding and migratory areas. The Whaling Convention Act was repealed in 1982 and replaced with the Cetacean Protection Regulations. The Regulations stated that "anyone, other than Indians and Inuit, wishing to hunt cetaceans must obtain a license from the Minister of Fisheries before doing so." Natives could hunt whales (except for right whales) only if the whales were used for local consumption. These Regulations were replaced by the Marine Mammal Regulations of 1985, which were amended in 1993. Under the Regulations, all disturbance of marine mammals is prohibited, including "repeated attempts to pursue, disperse, and herd whales and any repeated intentional act of negligence resulting in the disruption of their normal behavior." In 1996, the federal government passed the Canada Oceans Act, which gave the federal Department of Fisheries and Oceans (DFO) the final responsibility for Canada's oceans. It also gave the DFO the power to establish marine protected areas to conserve marine species and the power to establish emergency protected areas in cases where species or systems are under severe threat.

All three nations are to be congratulated for their farsightedness in helping to conserve one of the ocean's most magnificent animals.

Chapter Five   On the Horizon

There will be nothing left of this gigantic species but a few vestiges ... It will live on only in human memory.
    – Comte de Lacépède, 1804

A year ago, I found myself sea-kayaking in the sparkling waters of Kennedy Inlet on the western coast of Vancouver Island. A harbor porpoise swam for a short distance alongside me, and the soaring dowrsal fins of three killer whales hugged the rocky shore. Above me, a lone bald eagle screamed his defiance at my intrusion into his pristine domain. But my little bit of paradise was ruined by what I found in the little bay where I beached my kayak: two beer cans, a bleach bottle, and the torn shards of a fishing net.

During a meeting of the American Cetaccan Society in 1990, Charles Mayo of the Center of Coastal Studies in Provincetown, Massachusetts, sounded a cry of alarm concerning the fate of the world's oceans, saying "we treat the richest ecosystem on our earth not as our garden but as our dumping ground." According to the Canadian Department of Fisheries and Oceans, "more than 80 percent of marine pollution comes from human activities on land." Much of the waste oil, solvents, and sewage that we thoughtlessly flush down our drains eventually ends up in the ocean.

Because toothed whales are at the top of the food chain, their bodies accumulate the poisons that pass up through that chain, becoming more and more concentrated along the way. Baleen whales are farther down the chain, so theoretically they don't show the effects of toxins as quickly. However, because gray whales migrate very close to shore, they are one of the first marine animals to show the effects of coastal pollution and marine traffic.

FACING PAGE: *This five-year-old gray whale washed up dead near Santa Cruz, California, entangled in a fishing net.* (Frank S. Balthis/ Nature's Desgin)

Unfortunately, a number of large port cities, including Vancouver, Seattle, Los Angeles, San Francisco, and San Diego, lie along the migratory path of the gray whale, spewing untold tons of waste into the ocean each year. Vancouver alone dumps over 756 million liters (200 million gallons) of sewage *every day* into the ocean. And even though most of it is treated, a recent survey found fifty-seven synthetic organic compounds on the bottom of Vancouver harbor. Three-quarters of the harbor's bottom-dwelling sole population have developed tumors or liver lesions.

In 1969, the blubber of one California gray whale was found to contain 0.50 ppm of DDT, washed into the ocean from coastal agricultural operations. Another was found to contain 0.075 ppm of dieldrin, an agricultural insecticide. The world's largest dump of DDT, over 220 tonnes (200 tons) worth, lies in the waters off the Palos Verde Peninsula in California, right along the gray whale's migratory path.

In the late 1980s, a number of dead gray whales washed up in Puget Sound and the Strait of Georgia. An autopsy on one of the whales showed "measurable contaminants" in the whale's tissues, although no exact cause of death could be determined. It is not known what level of toxins are lethal to gray whales, but the number of dead whales found with measurable quantities of toxins in their tissues is a matter of some concern.

Oil spills off both California and British Columbia also pose a potential threat to gray whales. After the *Nestucca* oil barge spilled 875,000 liters (231,000 gallons) of oil off Vancouver Island in 1988, biologist Jim Darling found oil in every one of fourteen random bottom-sediment samples. As a bottom-feeder, the gray whale is especially susceptible to ocean-bottom pollution.

No grays apparently died as a result of the 1969 Santa Barbara and 1989 *Exxon Valdez* oil spills, the two biggest oil spills off the western coast of North America so far. And historically, grays have traditionally migrated through the Santa Barbara channel for centuries, where naturally occurring oil seeps have caused them no apparent harm. But Unimak Pass, the small Aleutian Island pass through which thousands of grays migrate each year, received one of the highest impact ratings in a 1975 oil spill model study. What would happen to the gray whales if a real oil spill occurred there?

Even though the effects of pollution have been trumpeted to the world for three decades, many ships still use the ocean as a giant garbage can. According to one 1985 study, merchant ships dump 450,000 plastic containers into the ocean every day. David List, of the US Marine Commission, describes this trash as "individual mines floating around the ocean just waiting for victims."

In 1997, four dead gray whales washed up near Culiacan, on the mainland coast of Mexico east of Cabo San Lucas. Autopsy results on the animals were inconclusive, but the Group of 100, a Mexican environmental organization, believes the whales died from a poison called NK-19. This cyanide-based chemical glows red in the daytime and blue at night, and is used in Mexico by drug smugglers to mark drop-off points for contraband at sea. In addition to the gray whales, the corpses of seventy-two dolphins and whole schools of dead sardines have been found in the area.

A more insidious threat lies under the water of the Farallon Sea, off the northern coast of California. The site is used to dispose of nuclear waste and unfortunately is just west of the Gulf of Farallon, where a number of gray whales spend their summers.

At the water's surface, the huge number of boats and ships off the west coast poses a serious physical obstacle to migrating grays. San Diego biologist Ray Gilmore once found five gray whales whose tails had been cut off by boat propellers. One tailless gray left the San Diego area on February 14, 1958, arriving off Kodiak Island, Alaska, on May 3. His trek averaged forty to fifty miles a day, half the normal rate of speed, but an amazing achievement for a tailless whale. To prevent such disasters from occurring during the breeding season, Mexican authorities in Baja do not allow marine traffic close to shore.

Discarded fishing nets pose yet another hazard to gray whales. As air-breathing mammals, grays must be able to position their blowholes so that they can take in air. Only a few minutes of entanglement in a fishing net can spell death to a gray whale. In 1980, biologists with the Russian whaling ship *Zvezdnyi* reported taking one or two whales per year which had "remnants of synthetic ropes, fishing nets, etc." on their bodies. They noted that all of these whales were large adults which could free themselves from entrapment; younger animals probably weren't as lucky. Between November 1980 and June 1985, thirty-three grays were found entangled in fishing nets between San Francisco and San Diego; nineteen died.

Crab-pot lines are yet another obstacle that gray whales must learn to avoid. At least one gray whale near Tofino, British Columbia, has been spotted with a crab-pot line trailing from its mouth, which may interfere with its ability to feed.

One unusual threat faced by breeding whales in Baja is lagoon-side salt plants. Large areas of lagoons in Baja have been closed off to allow salt to evaporate from the pans, for the hot, dry climate and constant winds produce the perfect conditions for salt evaporation. Adjacent to Guerrero Negro Lagoon alone there are 688 square kilometers (300 square miles) of salt pans. Within Scammon's Lagoon, there is only one major channel that is not used by gray whales, and it is used several times daily by salt barges. Baja California produces a third of the world's salt, almost five million tons per year. Construction of salt-extraction plants in the area first began in 1956. Constant dredging to keep the main channel in Guerrero Negro Lagoon open apparently drove the whales from the area between 1964 and 1970. Following the departure of the salt company and its boat traffic in 1967, the grays returned to the lagoon.

In 1996, Mitsubishi, the giant Japanese conglomerate, and the Mexican Ministry of Trade announced plans to build the world's largest salt factory adjacent to San Ignacio Lagoon. The plans are being vigorously opposed by the Natural Resources Defense Council, which is collecting protest letters to send to the presidents of Mitsubishi and Mexico. Under the plans, over 23,000 liters (6,000 gallons) of water per second would be pumped into adjacent evaporation ponds, potentially altering the lagoon's temperature and salinity. The whales would have to negotiate around a 1.5-kilometer (1-mile)-long pier which would take salt by conveyor belt across the lagoon to container ships.

Biologists have condemned the joint venture's environmental impact statement as a complete joke, for it dismissed the lagoon area as "complete wastelands, with little biodiversity and no known productive use." Although it is hard to believe that Mexico would go along with the plans, the country stands to collect millions in export fees from the proposed factory. Most of the salt produced would go to Japan.

In addition to floating pollutants, effluents, and boat traffic, noise pollution is becoming a significant problem to whales and other marine creatures. Whales today face a barrage of human-generated sound from shipping traffic, seismic activity, and other sources. As whale biologist Katherine Payne says, "Whales are acoustic animals. Their lives are informed not by what they see but by what they hear." And increasingly, what they hear is a roar of human-generated noise.

In 1968, Jacques Cousteau observed gray whales via a small Cherokee 300 airplane, but "the racket from its engine quite obviously upset and frightened them." Today, most of the noise that grays hear comes from boat traffic. Hundreds of thousands of ships each year cruise along the western coast of North America. Over a hundred supertankers travel the oceans every day, along with thousands of freighters, tankers, and smaller ships. The noise from this traffic is bound to affect the sensitive ears of whales; belugas have been observed swimming seventy-five kilometers (50 miles) out of their way when they hear icebreaking vessels approach. A recent study found that gray whales changed course to avoid noise levels of 120 decibels, much quieter than the average outboard motor. (Supertankers produce a noise level of about 232 decibels.)

Off the coast of California, seismic survey vessels use underwater explosives in the never-ending search for new oilfields. In the Arctic, bowhead whales have been observed to change direction when such blasts take place in their waters. How gray whales react is unknown.

Other oceanic sounds originate with military tests. The US Navy is currently testing a new sonar system called Low Frequency Active Sonar, with which they hope to detect submarines by sending low frequency sounds through the water. Unfortunately, low frequency sounds are those which fit within the gray whale's range of hearing.

Ironically, other ocean sounds emanate from the projects of well-meaning marine biologists. Since 1995, Scripps Institute of Oceanography has been involved in a project known as Acoustic Thermography of Ocean Climate. The project involves broadcasting low frequency sounds from California to New Zealand to measure temperature changes in the Pacific Ocean. But the blasts of sound travel right across the gray whales' migratory path, and conservationists protested loudly when the plans were first announced. As a result, Scripps moved loudspeakers to a greater depth of

Humans have long treated our waterways as dumping grounds. (Robert H. Busch)

about 1,000 meters (3,200 feet), and changed to a different frequency (75 Hz). The project is now being closely monitored to determine any negative effects on sea life.

Sylvia Earle, a biologist formerly with the National Oceanic and Atmospheric Administration, is critical of the growing noise level within the oceans. "Each sound by itself is probably not a matter for much concern," she says. But added together, "the high level of noise is bound to have a hard, sweeping impact on life in the sea."

Some of that impact may be shown by recent changes in gray whales' migratory routes. Steve Swartz has reported that "in the last decade or so the animals are beginning to abandon routes in close to shore, within a mile or two." Two other researchers reported in 1979 that there was evidence the migration route of grays around Monterey had shifted farther offshore. Are we chasing them away with marine traffic, inshore pollutants, or high levels of noise? Or are most grays adapting to the noise and learning to ignore it? In 1997, I watched a young gray whale in Grice Bay near Tofino, British Columbia, which was surrounded by a semi-circle of six tour boats, all with their motors idling. Although the whale spy-hopped once and took a look at his visitors, he did not seem bothered in any way by the noise that surrounded him. This was a resident whale, though, an individual that had returned to the same area each summer for three years. Would other gray whales react the same way?

Perhaps gray whales are simply too "cool" to react strongly to boat noise. Grays have tiny adrenal glands, which are the organs that secrete adrenalin, a hormone pumped into the blood at times of stress, fear, or anger. The small size of the adrenal glands suggests that grays should be basically gentle and calm, difficult to arouse emotionally.

Studies of bowhead whales found that although they initially fled from seismic noise, dredges, and vessel disturbance, they usually returned and went back to their normal activities. Jim Darling has reported that humpback whales wintering off Hawaii have also become used to the heavy boat traffic around Maui. However, every species has its limits. It has been suggested that the apparent abandonment of the Glacier Bay area of Alaska by humpbacks in 1978 was due to the dramatic increase in whale-watching and tour-boat traffic in the bay.

The effects of all these marine problems are especially distressing when one considers the value of oceans to human as well as whale life. Oceans provide the main source of protein for almost half of all the people on Earth. They provide more oxygen than rain forests. Over two-thirds of the world's human population lives within eighty kilometers (50 miles) of the ocean, and nearly half of the largest cities on Earth are built on coastal sites. In a very big way, what we do to the whales by harming the oceans, we do to ourselves.

The Future of the Gray Whale

Off the west coast of Canada, the only large whales regularly seen besides grays are humpbacks. The blue whales, sei whales, finbacks, and right whales have all but disappeared, the victims of overhunting by whalers. As recently as 1965, 604 sei whales were caught off the BC coast, but that abundance of whales is now a thing of the past.

So why has the gray whale survived? Much of its success is due to its physiology. For one thing, the gray whale does not provide as much whale oil as blue whales, sei whales, finbacks, or right whales, so it was not pursued as relentlessly by whalers. It doesn't taste good, so it is not in favor by Asian gourmets. It doesn't compete for the same foods as humans eat, and its generalist feeding habits perhaps make it more flexible when certain food items are in short supply. And until the past twenty years or so, its breeding lagoons have been remote and rarely visited, hiding it from the greatest predator of all—mankind.

But what is to be the future of the gray whale? One of the most serious new threats to wildlife the world over is global warming, which is expected to warm the oceans of the world by two or three degrees over the next few decades. "This will have an enormous impact on the food of gray whales," says biologist Jim Darling. But neither Darling nor any other biologist I spoke to is willing to go out on a limb and predict how the gray whale will react to changes in its foods or food availability.

"The problem is that the feeding behavior of the gray whale is extraordinarily complex," says Darling. "And gray whales are a pretty tough bunch, pretty flexible in their feeding habits."

Will global warming result in superheated Baja lagoons too hot for gray whales? Or will the tough, flexible grays adapt and survive? Their home waters already range from the ice-cold Arctic waters to luke-warm lagoon waters; maybe a few more degrees of warming won't hurt them. No one knows.

Over the past hundred years, the gray whale has proved to be a remarkable survivor. In fact, it has not only survived, but has thrived. It is the only Pacific whale species whose numbers have increased dramatically since the height of the old whaling days. So perhaps it will always be here, summering in the Arctic and trekking south each winter to breed and give birth.

In *Moby Dick*, Herman Melville wrote an elegant passage that may well apply to the future of the gray whale: "If ever the world is to be again flooded … then the eternal whale will still survive, … spout[ing] his frothed defiance to the skies." We can only hope that Melville's optimistic prediction will come true and that the gray whale, the wandering giant of the Pacific, will always cruise its wild blue waters.

Bibliography

Anderson, Charlie. "The return of the harpoon." *The Vancouver Province*. April 20, 1997. p. A10-11.

Austin, Ian. "Natives, greens clash over planned whaling." *The Vancouver Province*. April 14, 1997. p. A5.

Banfield, A.W.F. 1974. *The Mammals of Canada*. Toronto: University of Toronto Press.

Bergman, Charles. 1990. *Wild Echoes: Encounters with the Most Endangered Animals in North America*. New York: McGraw-Hill Publishing Company.

BC Atlas of Resources. 1956. Vancouver: BC Natural Resources Conference.

Carwardine, Mark. 1995. *Whales, Dolphins and Porpoises*. London: Dorling Kindersley Limited.

Clutesi, George. 1969. *Potlatch*. Sydney, BC : Gray's Publishing Ltd.

Cousteau, Jacques-Yves and Philippe Diole. 1972. *The Whale: Mighty Monarch of the Sea*. New York: Doubleday.

Cousteau, Jacques-Yves and Yves Paccalet. 1986. *Whales*. New York: Harry N. Abrams, Inc.

Darling, Jim. 1988. "Whales: An Era of Discovery." *National Geographic*. 174(6): 872-908.

—. 1990. *With the Whales*. Minocqua, WI: NorthWord Press.

Day, David. 1987. *The Whale War*. Vancouver: Douglas & McIntyre.

Forester, Joseph E. and Anne D. 1975. *Fishing: British Columbia's Fishing History*. Saanichton, BC: Hancock House.

Forsyth, Adrian. 1993. *A Natural History of Sex*. Shelburne, VT: Chapters Publishing Ltd.

Francis, Daniel. 1990. *A History of World Whaling*. Markham, ON: Penguin Books Canada Ltd.

Fromm, Peter J., ed. 1996. *Whale Tales*. Friday, Harbor, WA: Whale Tales Press.

Goley, P. Dawn and Janice M. Stapley. 1994. "Attack on gray whales (Eschrichtius robustus) in Monterey Bay, California, by killer whales (Orcinus orca) previously identified in Glacier Bay, Alaska." *Canadian Journal of Zoology*. 72(8): 1528-1530.

Gordon, David G. and Alan Baldridge. 1991. *Gray Whales*. Monterey, CA: Monterey Bay Aquarium Foundation.

Gormley, Gerard. 1990. *Orcas of the Gulf: A Natural History*. Vancouver: Douglas & McIntyre.

Grenier, Robert. 1985. "Excavating a 400-year-old Basque Galleon." *National Geographic*. 168(1): 58-67.

Hagelund, William A. 1987. *Whalers No More*. Madeira Park, BC: Harbour Publishing Company Ltd.

Hall, Howard. 1985. "Eye to Eye With a Gray Whale." *International Wildlife*. 15(3): 3033.

Hoyt, Erich. 1981. *Orca: The Whale Called Killer*. Camden East, ON: Camden House Publishing.

—. 1984. *The Whales of Canada*. Camden East, ON: Camden House Publishing.

—. 1984. "The Whales Called 'Killer'." *National Geographic*. 166(2): 221-237.

Island of Whales. 1990. National Film Board of Canada film production.

Johnson, Kirk R. and C. Hans Nelson. 1984. "Side-Scan Sonar Assessment of Gray Whale Feeding in the Bering Sea." *Science*. 225(4667): 1150-1152.

Jones, Mary Lou and Steven L. Swartz. 1984. "Mothers and Calves: From Winters Spent Among the Gray Whales of San Ignacio Lagoon." *Oceans*. 17: 11-16.

Jones, Mary Lou, Steven L. Swartz and Stephen Leatherwood, eds. 1984. *The Gray Whale: Eschrichtius robustus*. New York: Academic Press, Inc.

King, Jane. 1989. *British Columbia Handbook*. Chico, CA: Moon Publications, Inc.

Laxalt, Robert. 1985. "The Indominable Basques." *National Geographic*. 168(1): 69-71.

Mallonée, Jay S. 1991. "Behaviour of gray whales (Eschrichtius robustus) summering off the northern California coast, from Patrick's Point to Crescent City." *Canadian Journal of Zoology*. 69(3): 681-690.

Martin, Anthony R. 1990. *The Illustrated Encyclopedia of Whales and Dolphins*. London: Salamander Books.

McHugh, Kathleen, ed. *Fodor's 1990 Mexico*. New York: Fodor's Travel Publications, Inc.

McNally, Robert. 1981. *So Remorseless a Havoc*. Boston: Little, Brown and Company.

"Mexican Deathwatch." *Canadian Wildlife*. (June, 1997) 3(2): 44.

Miller, Tom. 1975. *The World of the California Gray Whale*. Santa Ana, CA: Baja Trail Publications, Inc.

Montgomery, Sy. 1997. "From Sea to Noisy Sea." *Animals*. 130(2): 22-27.

Mowat, Farley. 1984. *Sea of Slaughter*. Toronto: McClelland & Stewart.

1993 World Resources Institute Environmental Almanac. Boston: Houghton Mifflin Co.

Nollman, Jim. 1987. *Dolphin Dreamtime: The Art and Science of Interspecies Communication*. New York: Bantam Doubleday Dell Publishing Group.

Obee, Bruce. 1992. *Guardians of the Whale*. Vancouver: Whitecap Books Ltd.

Pascua, Maria Parker. 1991. "Ozette: A Makah Village in 1491." *National Geographic*. 180(4): 38-53.

Payne, Roger. 1995. *Among Whales*. New York: Scribner's.

Quammen, David. 1988. *The Flight of the Iguana: A Sidelong View of Science and Nature*. New York: Bantam Doubleday Dell Publishing Group.

"Rare Killer Whale Attack." *1992 Earth Journal*. Boulder, CO: Buzzworm Books.

Reeves, Randall R. and Edward Mitchell. 1988. *Cetaceans of Canada*. Ottawa: Department of Fisheries and Oceans. 26 pp.

—. 1988. "Current Status of the Gray Whale, Eschrichtius robustus." *Canadian Field Naturalist*. 102: 369-390.

Reynolds, Susan. 1997. "Dooming a Whale's Last Best Birthplace." *Audubon*. 99(4): 18.

Stauble, Ann M. 1997. "Newsscan." *Animals*. 130(2): 15.

Steinbeck, John. 1941. *The Log from the Sea of Cortez*. New York: The Viking Press.

Stewart, Darryl. 1981. *The Canadian Wildlife Almanac*. Toronto: Lester & Orpen Dennys.

Stewart, Frank, ed. 1995. *The Presence of Whales*. Seattle: Alaska Northwest Books.

Swartz, Steven L. and Mary Lou Jones. 1987. "Gray Whales: At Play in Baja's San Ignacio Lagoon." *National Geographic*. 171(6): 754-771.

Tuck, James A. 1985. "Unearthing Red Bay's Whaling History." *National Geographic*. 168(1): 50-57.

Turbak, Gary. 1993. *Survivors in the Shadows: Threatened and Endangered Mammals of the American West*. Flagstaff: Northland Publishing Company.

Walker, Theodore J. 1971. "The California Gray Whale Comes Back." *National Geographic*. 139(3): 394-415.

Watching Whales. Ottawa: Department of Fisheries and Oceans. 1983. 23 pp.

Watson, Paul. 1982. *Sea Shepherd: My Fight for Whales and Seals*. New York: W.W. Norton & Company.

Whitehead, Hal. 1985. "Why Whales Leap." *Scientific American*. 252(3): 84-93.

Wursig, Bernd. 1988. "The Behaviour of Baleen Whales." *Scientific American*. 258(4): 102-107.

Zahn, Kara. 1988. *Whales*. New York: Michael Friedman Publishing Group, Inc.

Index